Milton

and

His Epic Tradition

Milton

and

His Epic Tradition

by

Joan Malory Webber

UNIVERSITY OF WASHINGTON PRESS

Seattle and London

Library of Congress Cataloging in Publication Data
Webber, Joan Malory
    Milton and his epic tradition.

    Includes index.
    1. Milton, John, 1608–1674. Paradise lost.
2. Milton, John, 1608–1674. Paradise regained.
3. Epic poetry—History and criticism. I. Title.
PR3562.W34   821'.4   78-4368
ISBN 0-295-95618-6

Joan Malory Webber

September 9, 1930–October 14, 1978

Joan Webber walked into my office one day in the late spring of 1958 and said to me, "I have an idea about Donne's *Devotions* and about his style. I want to write a book, not the usual dissertation. Can I do it? How do I do it?" She did it, not indeed without two further years of reading, thinking, and reworking what she presented to us as a dissertation, but the essence of the book was there from the beginning. The book was *Contrary Music: The Prose Style of John Donne,* winner of the Christian Gauss Award for literary criticism in 1963. Perhaps the most important thing Helen White and I did for her as directors of her dissertation was to sustain her in her initial vision. She was to go on to visions grander in scope—in a second book, *The Eloquent "I": Style and Self in Seventeenth-Century Prose,* and now in a third, this one on Milton and the whole epic tradition. In these and in her many articles she greatly fulfilled her wish to be a fine scholar—as she always too modestly put it, to be worthy of her teachers. Her modesty about her work stayed with her. No one ever listened more thoughtfully to criticism and suggestion, or more generously acknowledged help.

Her true mentor at Wisconsin was Ruth Wallerstein. With her, had she not died in an automobile accident in

England in early 1958, Joan Webber would have undertaken her study of Donne. She and Miss Wallerstein were kindred spirits in their intellectual passion, their acute sensitivity to nuances in style, their responsiveness to complex seventeenth-century minds and sensibilities. Joan Webber brought to her own work on that period a special quality of mind, which Helen White once described as an "unusual combination of delicacy of perception and discrimination of esthetic values." Those qualities together with her full and precise scholarship have brought her wide recognition as a distinguished interpreter of the seventeenth century.

One would like to say something about Joan's personality, her everyday self. But she was too complex to be summed up in a neat "character." Nothing about her was ever ordinary. She was not a self-regarder, nor did she live by the much-admired Ciceronian ethic of moderation and prudent reasonableness. She took life as it was offered, and with both hands. As she did in her scholarship and teaching, she participated intensely in everything she undertook, including marriage and motherhood. She was warmly loving, so generous that for a friend in need she would sacrifice herself without thought. As one might guess, she was a poet as well as a scholar.

My last memory of Joan is of her visit to Wisconsin in the fall of 1973. She gave a lecture in the English Department's graduate lounge on "The Literary Epic from Homer to Milton," which was to be the first chapter of her new book, to a packed audience of faculty, graduates, and undergraduates, many sitting on the floor. In a level, nondramatic style, hardly raising her voice, she went on for over an hour, and there was not a whisper or a rustle in the room. She held the young people spellbound, and they held her afterwards with many earnest questions and arguments.

In Colorado, where she did her first teaching and where she afterwards went for summer holidays, she fell in love with the mountains. It was partly that love which led her eventually to the Far West. Climbing became for her a special joy. On October 14 of this year she was killed in a simple climbing accident in Mount Rainier National Park. There had been no apparent danger, no lack of foresight on anyone's part. The accident was unavoidable, a casualty in the strictest sense. Joan left life unknowing, on a beautiful day, in a place she loved, her own beauty undiminished.

"Look how a bright star shooteth from the sky. . . ."

Madeleine Doran
The University of Wisconsin
Madison, Wisconsin
November 1978

For Rachel Elizabeth Markels Webber

Preface

This book had its origin in a study of Milton's God in which I tried to discover whether anything in classical epic would provide a context for the unorthodox theology of *Paradise Lost*. My conclusion was that epic is essentially, though often quietly, subversive. Whatever is assumed to be the informing purpose of any epic story, whether the Trojan war or the defense of fair ladies, provides not only the narrative but also a target for the author's criticisms of society. To the extent that a world view is attached to the story, it too is criticized. Obviously, Milton must intend us to look rather closely, in this tradition of subversion, at a God who accounts both for a good deal of the action and for the world-view of this poem.

The present book attempts to chart more fully the extent to which Milton's central concerns are compatible with those of earlier epic writers. I first attempted to read the poets of his tradition as if Milton had never existed: my interpretation of that tradition is given in Part I. To some extent, of course, the aim of such a project is disingenuous. Since I knew Milton better than any of the other writers, and since he himself dictated, either explicitly or implicitly, which writers belonged to his tradition, I could not really read Homer, Vergil, and Dante without awareness of the poet who was my reason for reading them. Nevertheless, I did try to set forth the chief common "ideas" of these poems without reference to their relative importance in *Paradise Lost* and *Paradise Regained*. This critical principle, faulty as it may have proven, was my only means to an objective reading, which would in turn allow me to compare Milton to his predecessors. My work in this respect was greatly facilitated by scholarly books devoted to one or more of these early writers. When my points of emphasis coincided with theirs, I had some evidence of the objectivity of my conclusions. After the "ideas" of these poems had been organized into the first section of the book, I provided epigraphs from *Paradise Lost* for each subdivision in order to acknowledge the (I hope) minimal awareness of Milton's presence which was intrinsic to the making of this section.

When epics are thus read, in a sequence, different kinds of patterns emerge from what one sees in considering them without particular reference to chronology. The most impressive is a portrayal of the history of human consciousness, and of significant changes in consciousness at crucial periods in history. Seen in this light, traditional epic characteristics, such as visits to the underground and epic battles, become the apparatus for the delineation of consciousness, rather than primarily adventures for their own sake. Thus I am setting forth what I believe to be a major enterprise of epic, without denying that this exceedingly rich form is open to many other kinds of readings.

Some of the limitations of this book are implicit in its intention. I am not defining a genre, but describing a tradition that the poets themselves have created and named. My study deals only with a very coarse, or large aspect of style, epic themes, rather than with those finer elements of grammar, metrics, phonology, and so forth, which require attention to the poems in their original languages. In fact, I am concentrating on the most readily translatable aspect of epic because that is what necessarily becomes central to a tradition which depends and capitalizes upon the exasperating but magical phenomena accompanying the movement and influence of poems from one idiom to another.

My work owes a great deal to numerous literary critics, both of the epic form and of individual epics. Because the task is invidious, one hesitates to name names, or to list more than a few of the most essential names, such as those of W. F. Jackson Knight, W. P. Ker, C. M. Bowra, and E. M. W. Tillyard. Certainly there are many more. In recent years the poems have been undergoing a process of re-evaluation that makes their continuing liveliness and importance much more evident, not only with relation to Milton, but also for our own time. Among critics whose work I have found helpful are Robert Durling, Thomas Vogler, Thomas Greene, John Steadman, and Joseph A. Wittreich, Jr. My most important and specific debts are given in the text. However, I might mention here that while significant scholarship exists on most of these poets, that concerning Vergil is particularly crucial. If Homer stands first in this tradition, Vergil invented the tradition as we know it, and several recent critics, such as C. J. Putnam and Mario DiCesare, credit him with making that tradition a subversive one.

I first began to study the epic in a faculty seminar with my colleagues in medieval and Renaissance studies at the Ohio State University. A similar group at the University of Washington enabled me to continue to learn and to test my ideas and my prose style during the writing of this manuscript. At different times, conversations about Spenser with John Webster and with Patrick Cullen have been of great value. I am grateful also to the members of a seminar on the epic which convened several years ago at the State University of New York, Binghamton, and which included many distinguished Miltonists who provided me with thorough and penetrating criticism of the description of epic which I was in the process of formulating. The manuscript has been read and carefully criticized, in whole or in part, by Charles Altieri, John Coldewey, Stavros Deligiorgis, James Kincaid, John Mulder, B. Rajan, John Steadman, and William Willeford. Almost every page of the book has in some way been improved by their criticism. Those errors which still remain must be ascribed to my intractability and not to their lack of care. My greatest debt, worthy of a dedication if that page had not been reserved for another kind of acknowledgment, is to Joseph A. Wittreich, Jr., who first suggested that I write this book, and who has read the manuscript at many different stages over a period of several years. It seems to me that I have now been discussing Milton with him for half a lifetime. This essay is a part of our conversation.

Contents

I

The Tradition

1. The Overarching Idea

Things unattempted yet in Prose or Rhime
[1.16]

This study was undertaken with the intention of describing a limited tradition of literary epic beginning with Homer,[1] of whose common concerns Milton was aware and which his awareness in turn helped to create. The word "tradition" is as important here as "genre": in fact, my study is not intended to define a genre for which the only universally accepted qualifying words are "long" and "narrative." [2] It is not even intended to define that part of the genre which is commonly called literary. It simply describes what is essential to this one Miltonic tradition, whose members fall together in such a peculiarly cohesive way that only with difficulty can they be considered apart from one another. In the course of writing this essay, I shall often speak of epic heroes, techniques, and so forth, and many of my comments have essential generic relevance. But such relevance can never be assumed here. I have only wished to show one tradition that Milton knew, and some ways in which his knowledge influenced his epic poems.

The poems in this line make it easy to believe that epic escapes whatever boundaries it may be assigned. In attempts to explain or describe its vastness, critics have said that epic is a comprehensive or encyclopedic form, that it must be qualitatively great, and that no one epic can be separated from its whole tradition. To consider such admittedly impressionistic terms is to see that epics like those of Homer and Vergil differ from other forms (and even from other epics) somewhat as mountains differ from hills. That there is such a thing as a mountain is obvious, although the dictionary can tell us only that it is larger than a hill, a distinction not always adequate. Just so, epic is a long narrative, but the *Aeneid* is something more.

An encyclopedic form, according to Northrop Frye, is one that encompasses the myths of a whole culture, probing the boundaries of Heaven and Hell: it is comprehensive in space and time, and in philosophy.[3] Lucretius and Ovid easily join with the Bible and Milton, as epic becomes one of a number of kinds in this group. But one can also think of its comprehensiveness generically: Homer's poems were supposed to be the sources of romance, satire, hymns, orations, epigrams, and histories, and subsequent poets consciously adopted inclusiveness as a technique.[4] Each literary kind produced and satisfied certain cultural expectations: epic was intended to satisfy all, and therefore must constantly be reaching out for wider scope and vision. Since there are certain expectations for epic itself, almost all of which are arguable but many of which are usually fulfilled, it is structurally possible for the genre to include lesser forms without emphasizing them: one need not be distracted by or even especially aware of all the elements of romance, comedy, psalm, hymn, debate, oration, and pastoral that are part of *Paradise Lost*.[5] Other epics partake so strongly of different genres that their own identity is less clear. For some readers, the *Faerie Queene* is a romance epic, in which neither one element nor the other seems dominant; Joseph Wittreich has recently given the poem a different perspective by calling it epic-prophecy.[6] So epic poems, committed to inclusiveness, shade almost imperceptibly into other forms.

More than other literary kinds, the epic seems almost defined by its supposed superiority. Aside from the common use of the word interchangeably with "great," a convention which inevitably sets up expectations when we think of epic poetry, the definition is ordinarily tested on a very small number of poems: no one uses second-rate epics for illustrations. There is an easy explanation for that: no one has time to read epics that are less than admirable, and so we define epic by Vergil, not by Statius or Apollonius of Rhodes. Almost automatically, then, greatness comes to be taken for granted. But the problem is not only a lack of world and time. As Brian Wilkie has observed, some critics have made greatness a criterion of the genre,[7] a demand that should seem absurd. But the poets themselves have accepted, perhaps even created the challenge. It is a way of acknowledging what seems always to have been considered the extreme and unique difficulty and sensitivity of the undertaking. Despite Aristotle's designation of tragedy as the higher form, the epic has become so nearly indefinable partly because it has with surprising regularity been reconfirmed as the poets' ideal poem, the almost inconceivable, much less achievable task. And because it is a characteristic of great epic to probe and extend the limits of human consciousness, we only know those that not only change, but even revolutionize the tradition. In some sense, then, we are trying to define a genre by a series of great poems each of which rejects the assumptions of its predecessors.

The third "transcendental" [8] characteristic of this epic

tradition is that, despite its typical rejection of its predecessors' assumptions, every one of these poems is organically related to every other member of its tribe. The series of poems that leads from Homer to Milton "operates through propagated family resemblances rather than in obedience to more abstract laws." [9] Catalogs, epic similes, bleeding trees, heavenly councils, and so forth are family traits, like birthmarks. Obviously, not every poem—or person— has them all, but they are always present in sufficient number, and in a significant enough constellation, to make the poet's intention clear. Of course they have their own intrinsic meanings, but the meaning that simply signifies the continuity of the form is of great importance to begin with because it is an announcement that no one of these poems can be understood apart from its tradition. These epics represent the family of western man. Their history seems almost as biological as that of evolution itself: part of the excitement of great epic is that we always see in it a consistently recognizable pattern of human consciousness in conscious competition with the past.

In this line of poems, then, acceptance into the canon is dependent on genealogy; a poem little affected superficially and substantially by its specific predecessors and/or successors does not belong. All genres of course reflect the human condition, and one can trace it, and humanity's awareness of itself, through any enduring form. To give a recent example, Laurence Stapleton's *The Elected Circle* very precisely describes the changing nature of our self-awareness, by analysis of a series of literary essays written over a period of three hundred years.[10] But Stapleton was able to make arbitrary choices of the best or most interesting material, and had no need to indicate any conscious relationships among the different writers. Obviously, essays resemble other essays; elegies, like epics, have identifying characteristics. But the line which *de facto* constitutes the western tradition of literary epic is unique in its tightly genealogical and stylistic sense of responsibility to itself. By its behavior it has created and policed its own heritage.

In discussing the "diffuse" epic, Milton explicitly mentions the two poems of Homer, the *Aeneid*, and Tasso's *Jerusalem Delivered*.[11] Once those poems are given, it seems necessary, because the poets themselves have depended on one another, to include also the *Divine Comedy*, the *Orlando Furioso*, the *Lusiads*, and the *Faerie Queene*. The romance epics complicate definition, but it would be impossible to deny that *Paradise Lost* itself is a romance, or to suggest that Milton's lifelong debt to Spenser was in any way canceled by his decision not to write his own epic about Arthur. In previous studies of the epic, Dante, Ariosto, and Spenser have all been controversial, with some critics accepting them entirely and others rejecting their legitimacy. All of them include romance elements; in addition, prophecy in the *Divine Comedy* and the *Faerie Queene*, and irony in *Orlando Furioso* have an uncommonly important place if one is thinking of epic as necessarily a spare and rigorous heroic form. Yet any such attempt at definition limits the author too much: he has to be free to explore any region of the mind, directed only by his own acceptance of the known role of epic poet. In other words, it is just the "diffuseness" of epic, in its capacity for encyclopedic choice, that enables it accurately to represent the human mind at any stage while still maintaining its own tradition. And the poets, not the critics, identified their predecessors. Each poem, given its epic heritage, specializes in a different way, comprehends in a different way the nature of consciousness.

Since the epic poet's task is to transform the past into the future, he is responsible, so to speak, to carry on the family name. At the same time, he obviously must in some way reject the past as unequal to provide the skills necessary to construct the future. The ability to pay sufficient heed to the past while articulating a new stage of consciousness distinguishes the great or the essential epic from those that are identifiable merely by the traditional stylistic and thematic characteristics. There cannot be very many great epics because, once that change in consciousness has been recorded, the task has been accomplished for its time. Only in periods like the Renaissance, of extreme change or many-sided genius, can more than one significant epic be produced.

Each epic poet, in learning his craft, has an almost impossibly high level of excellence to look back to, but it is also excellence of a kind not precisely relevant to his own needs. Not only could no one rival Homer; to try to do it on Homer's own ground was pointless, as evidenced in the literary remains of the poets who tried. Vergil's task was to transform Homer into a new idiom, as Troy had to be transformed, and as Aeneas, after learning all he could from Anchises, had to be born again. The sophisticated urban context of Augustan Rome called for a poem essentially different from the *Iliad* and the *Odyssey*, but one that could draw nourishment from what was already a tradition, an ancestry. Rome, with its strong sense both of piety and of mission, was an ideal environment for the first definitive witness both to the value of that ancestry and to the necessity of remaking it.

The belief that epic ended with Milton has its origin in a misunderstanding of the genre. It is certainly much harder since the nineteenth century for poets and readers to submit themselves to tradition and imitation in the way that epic poets and their readers must do. The modern concept of originality has restricted our thinking to such an extent that it seems impossible to do *anything* new. But in any case it is clear when we read Dante and Milton that, despite (and because of) the great technological changes that have taken place, we are still living in the Renaissance, and it may simply be too soon to expect another poet of their stature. A tradition that was essentially created by means of a leap from the *Iliad* and the *Odyssey* to the *Aeneid* would have no particular difficulty with a hiatus between the seventeenth and the twentieth centuries. There is obvious evidence of new epic poetry in the intervening years, especially in the nineteenth century, when the Romantics reworked Milton's *Paradise Regained* into still more subjective myths of self. But *Paradise Regained* still stands on its own merits, by no means written for a time too late, as a viable, accurate witness for our own age.

2. Beginnings

There is a Cave
Within the Mount of God, fast by his Throne,
Where light and darkness in perpetual round
Lodge and dislodge by turns. . . .

[6.4–7]

Epic has consistently turned inward, pulled itself up by its own roots and started over, maintaining a hostile but loving responsibility to its rejected past. The intensity of its self-regard might seem antithetical to the claims it has made for divine inspiration, if these two characteristics did not have such obvious analogies with the very problems that are central epic themes. Consciousness, especially self-consciousness, is both a gift and a curse: how to accept and transcend without denying it is the human dilemma and the epic task. The inspired, self-conscious poet may be one with the hero of the poem.

The fall of man has often been interpreted as a fall into self-consciousness. But to repair the ruins of our first parents, which Milton saw as the task of education, is to heal and remake consciousness, not to deny it. The historical extension of consciousness has been described many times in remarkably similar terms. One might compare, for example, Erich Neumann's *Origins and History of Consciousness*, with Erich Kahler's *The Inward Turn of Narrative*.[12] Between these two very different works, there are important points of agreement. Both writers believe

that human consciousness has greatly expanded its territory during the course of time, but at serious cost. Neumann describes the process as one by which the personal
has of necessity asserted itself against the transpersonal,
and then rejected and denied its own origins. In Kahler's
terms, "by objectification of the outer world man takes
possession of his inner world" and "thus the dual process
paradoxically leads to an ever-intensified objectification
of both the outer and the inner worlds, and hence ultimately to an ever greater subjectification of the world. As
man objectifies himself he takes the world more and more
into himself, which is equivalent to the de-naturing of nature." [13] According to both critics, then, self-consciousness,
which has been identified with self-realization, also brings
about alienation. We become individuals, and thereby lose
our natural place in the world.

Both Neumann and Kahler see this process as historical,
a viewpoint which is acceptable if one recognizes that inherent consciousness is developed through its own inter-
changes with culture, not that the potentiality of consciousness grows with time. Further it is apparent that
from the beginning of knowable history the epic hero is
already a lonely human creature cut off from the pre-
historical collective existence of his past, denied entrance
into the elysium of the gods, and doomed to history as
mortality. Epic does not come into existence until it is
needed, that is, until consciousness has become apprehen-
sive, and articulate and sophisticated about its appre-
hensiveness. Yet it reaches farther back into that collective
past than any other form; from it we learn more than
from any other form about our emergence from that unconscious collective existence. Seen in this light, in fact,

the whole purpose of epic might be to find the way to some new and inexpressible meaning more satisfying than that which, because it was unconscious, was forever lost before it was recognized. A *Paradise Regained* ought to close the tradition, but cannot, because as long as men keep talking, there is a tension between their situation and their imagined goal. The *Paradiso* should have closed it too, but the narrator almost with his last breath holds onto words in order to tell his tale. Between the place where Odysseus weeps in Calypso's cave, and that where Dante's language begins to break, stretches the whole known history of western man.

From Homer to Milton, consciousness changes both quantitatively and qualitatively,[14] and the ways of describing it change. Yet any definition of literary epic that will work must begin with the fact of mortality,[15] and with the effort to deal with the sadness of this condition and the nobility of mortal striving toward self-transcendence. Epic is a form that uses myth to free men of history, even to the extent of making history itself part of the myth. It does not deny mortality, but by forcing mortality on people's awareness, by teaching them their own story in the form of myth that is more encompassing than history, it enables them to achieve transcendent vision.

The awareness of mortality begins when the mind begins to distinguish itself from its formless origins. Almost any kind of enclosed space stands in Jungian psychology for the unconscious or for the period in human existence when consciousness is just beginning to emerge: "Anything deep—abyss, valley, ground, also the sea and the bottom of the sea, fountains, lakes and pools, the earth, the underworld, the cave, the house, and the city—all are parts of this archetype." [16] So is the womb; but it is important to realize that this space which takes so many forms is limited neither to womb nor to female; those are limiting stereotypes given it by specific writers. In itself it is neutral and peaceful, and therefore almost necessarily not aggressively sexual. The concept of enclosure may already suggest man's effort to contain or suppress what really cannot be contained. As soon as this world begins to be recognized, to some extent it is lost because on the one hand it is made conscious and thereby objectified, and, on the other, suppressed and denied.

The cave and related figures are most useful for depiction of individual persons, while the underworld is more likely to hold the accumulated wisdom or myths of a civilization. Thus, Odysseus is alone with Calypso in the cave on Ogygia, but in the underworld he gives sacrifices to and learns from representativeness of his culture. The cave more frequently encloses passions; the underworld has knowledge of past and present. At best both are neutral places; at worst they are evil, and ultimately associated with the moral scheme of Christianity. In this part of my essay, I am primarily concerned with the implications of the cave. However, the same consciousness that sees a necessity to control the passions of the cave will inevitably in Christian times label some of these passions evil, and associate them with Hell. When this happens, the underworld has to enter the discussion.

Achilles' private space, his *klisiē*, which Richmond Lattimore translates "shelter," is the first epic cave in this tradition, and portrays perhaps better than any of the others the nature of the symbol. For more than any other character in the *Iliad*, Achilles is subject to a full range of human, yet, by our standards, imperfectly comprehended impulses. More than any of the other Greeks or Trojans, he is pulled this way and that by the gods, who in part represent men's own passions not yet internalized. When Achilles retires to his shelter, it is because he is angry and because, unlike all other characters in the poem, he does not deal with his anger in a primarily social, even ritualized fashion. Although he is more primitive in his impulsiveness than the others, he is for that very reason more in touch with the multiplicity of human feelings and possibilities. To think these out is fairly well beyond his capacities: he cannot come to any cool decision about whether to choose a long life or death in battle.[17] The way in which he confronts these issues gives us a very clear picture of a man at the cave's mouth, wholly in touch with himself, but with very little power of objectification. In contrast with Achilles, Hector, the city man, responds to challenges almost by rote, according to learned codes of loyalty and pride. The two men represent opposite extremes of human consciousness, the one all uncontrolled immediacy, the other with instincts so well channeled or suppressed that although he represents what is most noble in civilization he obviously also shows its fatal limitations.

Odysseus could be said to have found a midpoint between these extremes, for his highly developed consciousness carries him successfully through the war, and then he makes for himself a space, in the light of that consciousness, to re-experience the cave, in a wide variety of forms, beginning with the earliest. For us, the story of Odysseus begins on Ogygia,[18] although it is important to recognize that he himself does not. His story is neither a bildungsroman nor a chronological history of man. Odysseus does not change or grow up, but simply explores the self he has always been. With these qualifications, it is impossible to ignore the significance of the *Odyssey* as a symbolic tour of the mind and affirmation of human consciousness.

Calypso's cave is a neutral place: neither good nor bad, it is identified both with life—Ogygia is the navel of the sea—and death; located in the west, the island is filled with death-symbolizing flowers, trees, and birds. In other words, life and death are not yet even fully distinguished from one another, and in his state of diminished consciousness Odysseus cannot leave without help. Unhappy with Calypso, he nevertheless continues to sleep with her until she herself is forced by the gods (Hermes and Athena, especially associated with awareness and knowledge) to let him go.

Despite this significant lapse of attention, Odysseus does get home because he almost never lets himself lose consciousness, and in this respect he is clearly opposed to his men, who are vulnerable to Circe, the Cyclops, the oxen of the sun, the lotus, and so forth. It is obviously important for Odysseus to explore the dark places of the mind, but he does it almost always with alertness and self-control, as evidenced externally by his close connection with one goddess, Athena, who stands for conscious wisdom. Odysseus' acquisitive consciousness is to some extent a luxury, not essential to survival. He does not need to hear the sirens' song, and he several times sacrifices some of his men to his own curiosity, as in the episode with the Cyclops. More flexible, many-sided, and resourceful (aware of all the resources of human nature) than either Hector or Achilles, he tunes his mind to the enlargement of his world.

Yet, despite the stress on his wiliness, despite his loss of all his men, his destruction of the suitors, and his insistence that he cannot stop traveling even when he gets to Ithaca, he seems to be acting in obedience to a nature which he himself has not defined. He is conscious but not ego-centered. He makes choices with an eye to self-preservation and self-aggrandizement, but never questions his decisions or feels guilt or conducts any kind of self-examination. Despite, or perhaps because of, the aristocratic code upon which, from our point of view, he seems to depend, he may still be seen as the luckiest of men, having realized as much of human nature as can be had without undue suffering or self-denial. It is frequently argued (and Erich Kahler so argues) that there is no conscious symbolism in Homer,[19] and it is possible to believe this simply because the characters have no modern sense of self-awareness. Yet the symbolism, particularly that of the cave, is there, too insistent to be ignored. We find it hard to believe that Odysseus really understands what he does because he is so innocent of modern guilt: he can pay for knowledge with his own men, and still not have to worry about his soul.

There is no association of darkness with evil in Homer, one reason why the characters do not have to suffer "modern" kinds of confusion. By the time of Vergil that has all changed. Aeneas is extremely aware of duty, and therefore of moral oppositions. Odysseus is able to be playful even with the Cyclops; except for the Scherians, the whole poem seems to indicate that people who get killed are stupid or inconsequential. The ominousness of the marriage cave in the *Aeneid* and the sacrificial destruction of Dido present a much different psychic mood than that of the *Odyssey*. In the *Odyssey*, the dangers of unconsciousness are hardly menacing because the main characters never seem seriously imperiled. In the *Aeneid*, the threat is much more active, and associated with darkness and evil. For Aeneas, to found Rome is a moral act, requiring self-knowledge and self-control.

Consistently in the *Aeneid*, caves are enclosed violence —the Trojan horse, the cave of Aeolus, Aetna, Allecto's cave.[20] If the winds got loose, they would destroy the universe. The symbol of female as source is neutral in Homer: in the *Aeneid*, femaleness is associated with danger. The Trojan horse, its womb filled with soldiers, mounts the walls of Troy: even the rapist of the city is a female symbol. The cave of Aeolus is pregnant with raging winds; Carthage is a harbor with twin peaks; and Dido extends the cave of her passions into an inner court of her palace, which contains marriage bed, altars, and funeral wreaths. This heavy use of female sexual imagery in the first part of the poem not only emphasizes the urgency of Aeneas' need to escape his past, but also prepares us for the alliances between Turnus and women.

Calypso, ruler of the cave that in the *Odyssey* seems closed to the unconscious mind, is a protective and nurturing presence, who becomes a threat only to the extent that Odysseus wishes to assert himself. In the *Aeneid*, that threat is much more obvious, as the developing human consciousness increasingly suspects its source.[21] The Roman poem's heavy emphasis on order, duty, civilization, and control has polarized forces commonly identified as male and female, and labeled them civilized and wild.

Sea and storm imagery is connected to imagery of the cave, and the sea even has its own caves. But whereas the cave is something from which one may emerge, or which can be visited, the sea is an all-encompassing metaphor for life with its storms, and the need for self-control is evident. The sea can become a much more conscious experience for man than the cave. By an unequipped person the depths of the sea can be explored only so long as he can hold his breath. Essentially, the sea itself cannot be investigated; to be on it, to travel on its surface, one must be highly conscious, and aware of being supported by an alien element. It is in a way more dangerous and exciting than the cave: the self becomes aware of its situation, and of its own courage and unimportance.

The hero travels in a ship built by men. It must be steered between Scylla and Charybdis, it must stay afloat, it must be steered aright. Rage or lack of self-control is expressed by intentional burning of ships, lack of self-consciousness by sleeping while on duty. The classical poems are much more full of the sea than are the Christian ones; this is partly accidental, as other epics, like the *Lusiads* and the *Columbiad*, make clear, but water is an earlier, more originating figure, as well as an obviously necessary one for the stories those poems have to tell.[22]

Unlike Odysseus, Aeneas cares for his men, calls them comrades, and loses them only when they are chosen by the gods to be sacrificed. However, the kind of self-consciousness called forth by the Roman idea of duty does in a way seem to gain by losing. Odysseus loses his men without giving much thought to the fact; Aeneas accepts not only his responsibility for the welfare of others, but also the necessity of sacrifice, heavy self-discipline, and personal unhappiness. Yet just because all these characteristics are now present in the mind, whereas before they were not, Aeneas' Stoicism appears more culpable than Odysseus' obliviousness. It looks as though he is suppressing his own humanity even when what he suppresses are feelings of which Odysseus is not even aware. The idea of empire certainly changed man's consciousness, and its realization may have seemed to both Vergil and Dante essential to human order and dignity. But from those that it created, it demanded as much as it gave.

With Dante the figure of the dark wood becomes dominant over the sea as a means of expressing men's wayfaring.[23] Dante uses it briefly but authoritatively simply to express his own state of confused semiconsciousness at the beginning of the poem. The dark wood is threatening: its fierce animals represent man's own violent passions turned against himself. Later woods will be seen and used much more expansively, as places vast as the sea in which one can spend a lifetime wandering. Just like the sea, they are dangerous but not always destructive. The forest can be explored and understood.

Obviously what strikes us first about this opening episode of the *Divine Comedy* is that it is brief and that it is told by the person to whom it happened. Christianity has brought to psychology a new self-awareness and subjectivity; with Dante as hero we are given the character's thought-processes directly, and for the first time we do have something like a bildungsroman. The author subdues his own passions by learning what passions are.

The concept of the quest as spiritual becomes explicit; that is a characteristic of Christian narrative. Even though the Inferno, like the other parts of the universe of the *Divine Comedy*, represents the state of souls after death, Dante also says that allegorically his subject is man, liable to the rewards or punishments of Justice.[24] Dante explores the condition of these souls as a way of studying his own, and of escaping his own darkness. In Dante, as in Homer and elsewhere, people choose their destinies, and their choices are described by means of the transpersonal symbolism in which, for example, Aphrodite carries Paris away from danger in battle and puts him in his bedroom with Helen, or Ugolino, as punishment for his own sin of betrayal, is made to chew the skull of his betrayer. All that is familiar. What is new is that Dante's inner and bewildering dark forest (which itself, on one level, represents the objective dangers of evil in the world) is so quickly exchanged for an objectified general world inhabited by all sinners. These sinners may be thought of as having designed their own private caves of unconsciousness, figured in dark woods, fiery rain, deserts, coffins, or ice; almost none of them has any real awareness of his plight or even of the existence of his neighbors. Even if one sees Dante's descent into the underworld as a gradual objectification of his own unconscious, it is still in this respect unique in the tradition. Dante assumes the existence of an orderly Christian universe, and subordinates his personal darkness to the known and charted horrors of a Christian Hell. The distance which humanity has traveled in the course of three epics is made startlingly apparent by the fact that Odysseus, the explorer of caves, is now himself a prisoner.

Obviously one of Hell's major purposes is to persuade us that unconsciousness is sinful: to be in that condition is to be at the mercy of passions that prevent consciousness, and so human beings, newly emerged from the cave, are seen as lapsing back into it. But the cave that the mind chooses, enlarged by its own fantasies, is larger and more dangerous than it was in its original state. Dante responds to the dangers by naming them, that is, by enabling his readers to be absolutely aware of the name and place of every detail that would otherwise have remained vague and enchanting.

This does not, as some have argued, limit the seriousness of the undertaking. Ulysses is in the eighth circle partly because of his unquenchable desire for "full experience," and Dante's own need for full experience is the reason Vergil gives for taking him through Hell. The similarity of language is too close for comfort: it is difficult for any admirer of Odysseus to accept the idea that the one kind of experience blinds while the other enlightens. Just as Aeneas had to learn the discipline of obedience, Dante is learning self-government and self-knowledge through the subordination of himself to his own will. Ulysses used his will to get knowledge, not necessarily of self, and that, many centuries later, wrecked his ship on the cliffs of Purgatory. Explicit exploration of the meaning and possibilities of the will allows Dante to use Vergil as a base while pushing beyond him. A major tension in the poem is the exercising of Dante's will against the destructive pulls to pity and self-pity that the Inferno creates. Like Homer's Odysseus, he is (or becomes) one of the wholest persons in literature, but the undertaking is still filled with peril.

Also new in the poem is the persona's explicit dependence on language. It is not as though the story were being retold; it is relived through language, the experience is dangerous, and its outcome depends on Dante's ability to make the language do what it must—that is, to get the experience out of the character's mind and into the public domain. Where he himself fails to maintain control, or where language fails him, the tension of danger seems greatest. Dante faints—loses consciousness—when he loses perspective on his characters and experiences their weaknesses. When the language is not equal to the experience, it becomes doubtful whether he himself can survive and get back.

Just here is a crucial point. The language cannot be *equal* to an experience that is essentially sublingual. The language of Hell coarsens enough to give us an experience of bestiality. It cannot diminish enough to make us mindless unless it ceases to be. Dante is aware both that words cannot reproduce Hell, and that words are what make possible the consciousness that alone can carry him through it. He is the first epic writer to be aware of this dilemma, which is always a necessary part of exploration of the unconscious, whether or not the unconscious is associated with evil. At the bottom of Hell it is thus:

> How chilled and faint I turned then, do not ask, reader, for I do not write it, since all words would fail. I did not die and I did not remain alive. . . . [34.22–25]

And Canto 1 of *Purgatorio* announces the rising of the poetry from the dead. That he commits himself so much to his language, while always needing to live at the edge of its possibilities, brings Dante the character closer to Dante the poet and makes obvious the heroic undertaking of the poem itself.

Ariosto's poem is startling in the boldness of its iconoclasm, for it reduces Dante's whole design to less than two cantos, in which Astolfo chases the harpies into the underworld, and thereby, as it were by accident, embarks on his brief tour of Hell, the earthly paradise, and the moon. The harpies were punishing a king who tried to conquer the earthly paradise, and so Astolfo is enabled to see it by saving someone who had sinned against it. He finds the food in paradise so delicious that he cannot blame Adam and Eve for eating the apple. And Heaven is reduced to a moon that is a kind of warehouse for things lost on earth. Although Astolfo goes to the moon to get Orlando's lost wits, even that fact is telling: he is a courier, rather than, like Dante, a struggling human soul. He is chosen because he is the most unbelieving, the most unillusioned person in the poem. In the underworld, he learns nothing; in fact, he meets there only one person, a woman who had extensively punished an unwanted suitor. He did not need to leave the world of the poem to find her like. The whole trip is an obvious parody and rejection of Dante's experience. The only piece of wisdom given Astolfo here—and it is important—is that poetry creates value. He learns this in the moon, from St. John, and that is important too, for it denies the objective truth of the Bible, just as the whole sequence undercuts Dante's vision.

The amount of cultural change that Ariosto seems cavalierly to take for granted is so extraordinary that it may in itself account for the unwillingness of many critics to grant him epic stature. Dante's own edifice in its combination of sureness with subjectivity is the product of a unique mingling of luck and fortitude, history and chance. It says all there is to be said about an exceptionally brave and creative man's encounter with the medieval world. Perhaps more than any other epic it created a fully realized imaginative society both fragile (composed of "intelletto d'amore") and trustworthy (inhabited by solid historical beings). Dante needed it, and so did Italy. It is said to have created Italian culture.

Yet Ariosto takes no pleasure at all in his countryman's work; it seems to him to have been a waste of time. With the shrinkage of Dante's afterlife into two cantos, and the heavy reintroduction of an unreconstructed medieval world, Ariosto rejects the detached perspective that Dante achieved in the empyrean. For between Dante and Ariosto came the widespread European adoption of gunpowder and the death of heroic ideals. For Dante rectitude was an ideal that had been and was continually being fulfilled both on earth and in the full communion of the saints. It was something that one could taste, as evil could be kicked. For Ariosto, Satan's profanation of material things has wiped out the possibility of that kind of certitude. Value-free materialism is unavoidable, and its nature and effect are such as to render any coherent metaphysical system unattainable. The cave has taken over the world. The poem is filled with images of madness, dark woods, and storms. People never get where they intend to go, or stay where they belong. They are in conflict with themselves, at the mercy of others, and unsure of the value of any state of being or course of action.

As in Dante, and as explicitly, the poet is the hero. He denies all the help that other epic poets depend on: he has no muse, no Apollonian lyre, and he is miserably tied to a mortal love. He is entirely conscious of his own and all men's limitations, and he could not seem heroic otherwise. Yet he is the architect of his poem's world, absolutely in control, and he lets us know it by his many analogies with other arts, his explicit selection or rejection of certain characters and episodes, his explicit interventions in the poem on behalf of one or another character, his extraordinarily complex and faultless interweaving of plots, and his constant, blatant manipulation of the reader. Both characters and audience are dependent on his knowledge of the whole design of his art, for only the art makes sense out of chaos, and only artistic meaning is possible. Subjectivity thus has been carried a step further than in Dante, whose universe had a generally accepted universal justification. And the relationship between language and sanity is total. In the *Inferno*, there is a margin of grace. The poet in a faint or in a dream may be carried from place to place, revived, set going again, because of Beatrice and all that she represents. The very title, *Orlando Furioso*, signifies the vast space between the two poems. Ariosto's fictional hero cannot depend upon his sanity, not because he ever tries to approach the limits of meaning, but because the world has none. Beatrice saves Dante because justice and mercy exist. Ariosto saves Orlando because he wants to. Without the poet's magical words, Ariosto's world would seem at best a nightmare; with his pervasive ability to take nothing seriously except his art, it all seems funny and even exhilarating. We cannot learn our way out of our own ignorance. Words merely allow us to retain the consciousness that we create out of words.

Ariosto's story has in it a battle, which is won, yet in the welter of detail that battle, which ought to be the point, can go almost unnoticed. It is as apparent in Ariosto as it is in Dante that battles need not be the point of epic story, need not, in fact, even take place. But the cave is always there. So far that cave has been present in the origin of the hero; it has been a presence between him and his goal; and, in Ariosto, it has erupted into something that makes the goal itself apparently worthless. The cave can also become identified with the goal. The palace on Ithaca is both goal and threat, with Penelope as treasure and captive. In fact, it seems quite usual that, despite all the inner searching that the hero may do along the way, the most intense self-confrontation still remains at the end, as when Aeneas has to conquer himself in Turnus. The most blatant example of all is Tasso's *Jerusalem Delivered*, for here the city itself is the cave.

It is extraordinary that a band of warriors who have been six years in progress toward their goal should fall apart just when they arrive at the gates of Jerusalem. But that is the point of the story: the warriors lack inner unity and Jerusalem makes them confront (or, at first, run away from) themselves. However, despite Tasso's awareness of this truth, one is never convinced that he himself has seen all the implications of his tale.

It is commonplace that poems often contain more than their authors knowingly wrote into them. Because of their characteristically archetypal material and their open invocation of the power of the muse, one might almost say that epics advertise their transcendence of their authors' minds. Tasso himself provided an interpretation of the allegory of *Jerusalem Delivered:* the army is man, Jerusalem is civil happiness. Godfrey is understanding, and the other Christian princes are the other powers of the soul. The pagan sorcerers are servants of the devil, and the enchanted wood is "the variety and multitude of opinions and discourses of men." [25] And so forth. But while Tasso was an extremely skillful literary critic and theoretician, he was also at his best a brooding, subjective poet, with depths surely unavailable to his critical mind. He fought his own battle for sanity during much of his life: from the caves of his poem we can learn much that he must have repressed. Epics do not always show us heightened authorial consciousness, but they do get new material out of the unconscious and into words. As critics have noted, part of Tasso's peculiarly painful psychology is a preference of failure to success. His misogyny is extreme, but not simple. His poem has no winners, and some of its most moving episodes involve sympathetically portrayed pagan and female characters. Ariosto puts human misery on the surface and then laughs at it, impressing us with the power and necessity of awareness; Tasso has the opposite effect, introducing us to the inarticulate, distorted, yet hauntingly memorable depths of the soul.

Tasso's principal cave is the enclosed hostile city of Jerusalem, which is penetrated by means of a tower and destroyed so that it can be saved. This sacred female place is filled with the dark forces of the infidel; woman is both holy mother and destroyer. The most significant women in the story are pagans. Parallel with the fate of the city

is that of Clorinda, the most impressive of the pagan warriors. Like the city, she is Christian by heredity but not in
fact. She is loved unrequitedly by the Christian warrior
Tancred, who unknowingly deals her a deathblow in battle
and then baptizes her before she dies.

The other major female figure in the poem is a witch,
Armida, who overwhelms men with her beauty and then
turns them into fish in her pond. Clearly, for Tasso,
women are a supreme threat to male consciousness, representing both a primitive state of unconscious bliss (the
fish-pond), and the condition of fear and struggle with
the alien self. Tasso tries to find in Christianity a solution to everything, but the solution requires Armida's
self-abdication, and the deaths of both Clorinda and the
city.

Tasso also takes the animals of Dante's dark wood—
man's own passions—and elaborates them into a long and
highly subjective episode. When the first military tower
has been burned by Clorinda (who loses her life in this
passage), another one must be constructed, but an enchantment has been put upon the forest from which the
wood is to be procured. As various warriors in turn go
upon this quest, they are turned back by phenomena that
represent their own fears and passions. The strong are
vanquished by fear, Tancred by pity and guilt. Rinaldo
is tempted to passion and lust, but by this time has gained
the experience necessary to overcome his own weaknesses,
so that he can reclaim the forest for his army. Then, when
all those female wiles of magic and sex are seen through,
both the city and the witch Armida can be conquered.

In Jungian psychology, "female" is only one descrip-
tive word among many for the whole complex of material

associated with the unconscious, and the process of coming to consciousness is experienced identically by both men and women. That is to say, the sexuality of the cave, so far as can be known, is not a given of our collective origins. The varying emphases on its femaleness are the responsibility of individual writers. Tasso's poem makes uneasy reading; it is the product of a tortured mind in a highly repressive environment. He makes blatantly apparent that aspect of male nature that fears woman, associates her with caves, violence, unconsciousness, magic, and sexual passion, and would rather destroy the unknown than try to understand his fear of it.

Despite some obvious ineptitudes (such as the mingling of pagan and Christian deities), Camoens' epic, the *Lusiads*, seems much more sophisticated than Tasso's. It begins by repelling the modern reader in the same way. Tasso's army waged religious warfare. Camoens' Portuguese navy is embarked on a nationalistic venture that crudely combines religious fervor with the desire for empire, and it is difficult at first to penetrate that façade. But Vasco da Gama is given the mind of an explorer, and Camoens is sensitive to the complex combination, in exploration, of disinterested wonder with exploitative greed, as well as to the concept of self-conquest by means of exploration.

Portugal, like Britain, was noted for its ocean empire, and Camoens, recounting the story of how this empire came about, is entirely aware of its symbolic implications. In rehearsing the history of Portugal, he says that Joano I, bored because he had no more enemies to conquer, decided to pit himself against the ocean. Later the Ganges and the Indus, waters of the earthly paradise, appeared to Manoel in a dream, and he called upon Vasco da Gama to find them. The remarkably learned native king of Malindi compares da Gama's story to mythic assaults on heaven and hell:

"The giants in their arrogance made war on Olympus, if in vain. Theseus and Pirithous were bold, in their ignorance, to assault Pluto's dark and fearsome kingdom. If history records such daring enterprises as the laying seige to both heaven and hell, to assail the fury of the ocean is another no whit less hazardous or renowned." [Canto 2, pp. 75–76]

Ironically, one of the first signs of human resistance to da Gama has to do with water: when the Portuguese try to replenish their drinking water at Mozambique, the Moslems, stirred up by Bacchus, try to kill them. Bacchus, who is allied with the pagans, also tries to make common cause with Neptune, whose kingdom he says is being affronted by this voyage; so the winds are let out against da Gama's ships. And da Gama himself claims to have conquered the ocean.

Insistence on realism, on objective discovery, brings repercussions from the unconquerable unconscious. The sea lashes out at the Portuguese, not only in the storm raised by the winds, but also in the person of the giant Adamastor. His story is a telling one. In the great war of the giants against the gods, his task was to conquer the sea, and in particular he wanted, by force if necessary, the love of Thetis. Tricked by the nymphs into believing that she would give herself to him, he abandoned warfare and was then transformed into the Cape of Storms. He threatens da Gama with the authority not only of the unconscious, but of the whole underworld, predicting ills to come upon future Portuguese travelers of the sea.

Da Gama succeeds in facing down all oceanic perils, and from this point of view his work is enviably direct and simple. But while the sea is his own chief interest, Africa and India are Portugal's reason for sending him out. Camoens' epic ponders the problems of the inextricability of conquest and desire for fame from pure exploration. Da Gama himself is not interested in empire-building, but obviously he prepares the way for those who are. The second movement of the unconscious into the explorers' world is the final episode of the epic, when Venus builds them an island in the sea, inhabited by nymphs, to reward their labors. With unsteady but impressive grace, Camoens here attempts to resolve the conflicting impulses that motivate his hero.

The most important psychological recognition is that the true explorer can discover himself. Venus brings it about that the sea, which has shown so much hostility to the travelers, yields to them in love just because of the severity of their trials. Camoens says that this is a repetition of the trick Venus worked in Carthage to preserve Aeneas' safety, but in fact it is quite different, and the comparison serves to make us aware of the differences. For Aeneas, Carthage has to be merely a stopping-off place, and, inevitably, Dido is a pawn. Camoens does not bring his travelers back to Portugal. The Isle of Nymphs is their real destination, and the nymphs control the situation, choosing their lovers. The nymphs and mariners marry, internal and external become one, and the secrets of the universe are revealed to da Gama. The love passages are marked by extraordinary beauty and purity, quite different from any of the temptation scenes in other epic gardens. The spiritually fulfilling character of exploration is its own reward. The physical perils of the sea can only harm the mariners if they think in materialistic, acquisitive terms.

Camoens also tells us that the whole episode is a way of describing fame. That complicates matters by reminding us again of the ambiguous interests of the mariners and of the fact that, although the epic ends in the sea, the story of da Gama does not. The poem cursorily mentions the return of the mariners to Portugal, but it worries at length about the abuses of power that go with empire. For Camoens, fame is a plant that grows on mortal soil, and it is worth striving for. Even though he recognizes the corruption that accompanies all human endeavor, and has seen and is willing to report in his poem the degradation of his own country's empire, he cannot abandon the idea that obviously gave his own life meaning.

From the beginning, no epic, except perhaps Dante's, escapes ambiguity about itself and its proper focus. The central ambiguity involves tension between the psychological and physical careers of the hero. Spenser's epic structurally takes account of this, beginning with the simplest kinds of epic lines in the Christian allegory of Book 1 and the classical odyssey of Book 2, and proceeding through more and more deeply complex, infolded psychological studies in the later books. Even in the earliest cantos, things are never as simple as they look: Error is not abolished just because the dragon Error is killed. In the grand climax of Book 1, when Redcrosse wins his right to the name of St. George by killing the dragon that has ravaged Eden, his victory is made to seem rather hollow. Eager for sanctity, and courted in marriage, he is denied both conditions because his presence is still required in the world, where he must put in his time implicating himself in more bloodshed and violence. In other words, even in these early books, it is clear that physical prowess does not necessarily involve any kind of real accomplishment; human caves are deeper and darker than at first appears to be the case.

As Spenser's caves become more sophisticated, two things in particular distinguish them from their predecessors. First and most obvious is his rejection of much of the male-female stereotyping of the romance-epic tradition. In Homer, Dante, and Ariosto, there are of course plenty of precedents for female equality, and Ariosto in particular gave him specific models. But Spenser's poem is uniquely concentrated on love as itself an epic goal.[26] Like no previous epic writer, Spenser explores the idea that wholeness cannot be achieved without knowledge of one's sexuality and without acknowledgment that a bringing together of male and female (whether in couples or in one's own nature) is necessary to human wholeness. The different ways in which the knights who know Florimel refuse to admit this (and it is interesting that Arthur is no different from the others) are the reason why she is imprisoned in the sea. For them, the business of brave knights is to pursue fair ladies, and any indication to the contrary (that is, Florimel herself) has to be kept hidden from them, while false Florimel (a male spirit in disguise) ministers to their desires. Only when Florimel's lover Marinell is able really to hear her pain and understand her needs, and his own, can she be freed.

A similar situation obtains with Amoret, who, like Florimel, is beautiful, loving, and helpless. She is advertised for marriage, and carried off by Scudamore just because he wants something to do and is physically capable. She is thereupon kidnaped again by Busirane, who represents lust, and can only be freed from his lair by Britomart, a woman, while Scudamore is unable not only to help, but even to have enough patience to wait for the outcome. Freed then to recognize her own lust, she is recaptured by another denizen of lust's kingdom, and again requires rescue, this time by her own chaste sister.

Repeatedly the poem reverses the usual sexual pattern, presenting imagery of male physical force aimlessly dependent on happenstance to give it direction. In the best situations, these forces are often controlled by women or feminine powers: the crocodile of Isis, Mercilla's lion, and London's river Thames are underground, kept in caves, but not unacknowledged. They have been learned, valued, and subdued, their tides and passions understood. But the problem remains. In Book 6, one horrifying crisis after another erupts from the midst of the poem's most peaceful pastoral realm. In their extravagantly misogynistic parody of the dangerous female caves of the *Aeneid*, the marauding cannibals and brigands of the *Faerie Queene* seem almost comical, but Spenser means us to know that these characters are not really comical at all. The cannibals who cannot decide which part of Serena to eat first are not all that different from Arthur chasing Florimel into the sea.

The other way in which Spenser's caves are unique is in their emphasis on the mouth. In many instances, the threatening cave is the mouth of a beast. This figure serves to parody the womb-cave as used negatively in the tradition. At least as interesting, however, is the association of the mouth with its most purely human function. From that first encounter between Redcrosse and the Dragon of Error, Spenser emphasizes the danger of words. Epic has commented on language, and its own language, from the very beginning—that kind of self-scrutiny is one of its characteristics. Spenser is simply giving a new emphasis to the tradition.

There are all kinds of reasons for this issue to be raised at this time. Renaissance emphasis on the vernacular and on classicism caused awareness of errors made possible by language, or at the very least of the relativism that different linguistic systems can create. The printing press, an instrument of enlightenment, was commonly bracketed with gunpowder as source of all the woes of the age. Accessibility of print means accessibility of error, and awareness of diversity. Finally, for any Renaissance courtier, the ever-present human lusts for gossip and flattery were particularly unnerving. Spenser finally brings the reader to see that consciousness can be so manipulated as to blind him to his own condition. One can know too much, desire to know too much about all the wrong things, and so clog his mind with error and vanity that he might never have emerged from the cave of unconsciousness at all.

It is significant, then, that the last complete book of the *Faerie Queene* is the book of courtesy, whose principal adversary is the Blatant Beast, representing scandal, which is particularly dependent on language. This beast is described as a hellish monster, child of Cerberus and Chimera or Echidna. As in previous epics, it becomes obvious that repeated emergence from and re-entry into the cave

enlarges the darkness with human sophistications and re-
finements. Passions that take their toll in language have a
peculiar horror. During the course of Book 6, it is never
possible to be sure who will be safe from the Blatant Beast,
or why. Serena and Timias are told that they can heal their
own wounds by restraint of passion, but there seems no
very good reason why they, more than others, should have
been punished for their passion to begin with. The dangers of the cave, let loose in darkened language, appear to
have a kind of impersonal aimlessness to which almost any
human being may be vulnerable.

The Salvage Man, who is without language, is implicitly contrasted, for his virtue, with his linguistically
accomplished counterparts. He is incapable of some of the
subtle distinctions that get people into trouble; when he
sees vice, he never rationalizes it into virtue just because
it is clad in aristocratic garb. On the other hand, he is less
flexible than others in situations that may require tactful
understanding or mercy. Spenser allegorizes the problem
most explicitly at Turpine's abode, where Arthur chases
Turpine upstairs to Blandina's room, while the Salvage
Man kills people downstairs. Arthur decides, for Blandina's sake, to let Turpine live. He goes downstairs, stops
the killing, and brings the Salvage Man upstairs, where he
has to be restrained from killing Turpine. However, in
the next episode it is the Salvage Man with his club who
keeps the sleeping Arthur from being killed by Turpine.
Episodes like this one both mock and make use of the
whole history of the conscious and unconscious mind in
epic poetry.

There is no end to the story of the Blatant Beast, who
can be tied up but not killed, and who cannot even be

tied permanently. All human communication is corrupt because men are fallen, and mutual interest is always slightly tainted. The situation in Book 6 in which a couple innocently love-making are surprised by an innocent person simply walking along minding his own business exemplifies the problem. The encounter is embarrassing; complex reactions and motivations spring from nowhere. By the time he arrives at the end of Book 6, Spenser has convinced us that armed combat is not the way to kill vice, but he has not shown us that vice can be killed. Rather, he has demonstrated the fact that the cave is always with us, that we live with all kinds of caves, ancient and modern, and that while speech may give us our best defense against them, speech itself issues from a cave and therefore must be used with care.

In looking at this long history of man's treatment of the unconscious, one cannot exactly speak of a steady progression of awareness. That is one reason why it is so satisfying to conclude, temporarily, with Spenser, who shows all the varieties of awareness coexisting. And it is not just that by the time of Spenser, all this is available. All the material is present from the beginning. But the relationship between the human mind and its world does change as the mind becomes more or differently aware of itself and preoccupied with its own importance. In the Homeric world, where men and rivers can be literally related to each other, and rivers can rebel against being used as trashcans, obviously men need take less responsibility than when they themselves are the only conscious creatures. Vergil and Tasso also align people against each other morally, and in both these writers male and female are at odds. Vergil pits civilized against wild, and Tasso, Chris-

tian against Moslem. In Camoens, too, Christians are
turned against pagans; but, more importantly, men are
sent out to conquer the sea. All these writers know that
they are really describing men's struggles with themselves.
Dante knows this explicitly, and is the first to make his
epic literally a spiritual journey. His task is easier than it
might have been, because his moral map is so clearly organized. For Vergil, Ariosto, and Spenser, the power of
deception is greater than in the other writers. Although
they differ about whether truth exists or ought always to
be known, they agree that to know it is hard.

3. Subversive Form

Warrs, hitherto the onely Argument
Heroic deem'd. . . .

[9.28–29]

So far we have been looking at the hero's confrontation
of the unconscious as if it were itself (and it is) an epic
task. The usual method of dealing with epic is opposite
to this, to see the visits to dark places as stages on the
way to the goal. The epic has been supposed to be a celebration of a past time and of the hero who best exemplifies
its values, with the purpose of explaining or praising the
poet's nation. But the poet undermines the culture that he
seems to praise. Although he does not ordinarily suggest
that a better way of life is available, he does make clear,
with varying degrees of emphasis, that the available way

is, at the very least, extremely vulnerable to moral or social attack. Thus the constant straining to hold himself "above" the level of the cave is called in question not only by our uncertainty about the meaning of the cave itself, but also by a questioning of the civilized, rational values that the cave appears to threaten.

No simple patriot, the epic poet displays rather than celebrates his culture—on various levels, ambiguously, or in contrasting attitudes. One attitude is always celebratory; thus, critics who have seen the poems in this light were not wrong; they simply did not go far enough. Homer loves the world that he presents, and the words in which Vergil praises the virtues of Augustan Rome (6.852–53)—to spare the humble and put down the proud—have echoed too long in our western consciousness to seem insincere.[27] But both poets are very well aware that they are describing an imperfectible world in which ideals are not attained.

The *Iliad* obviously and unanswerably questions the value of the Trojan war. Hector and Achilles are the poem's heroes because they are both the most valorous and the most unwilling warriors. Helen, as the cause of the war, regrets her fate. The whole middle section of the *Iliad*, seen by many critics as too long-drawn-out and repetitious, performs the function of beating in upon our consciousness, in unsparing detail, the repetitious horror of warfare. One is never given a sense of Grecian triumph, only unremitting destruction, dissension, and, in the great climactic scene, the mutual sorrow of Priam and Achilles.

The historical necessity of the founding of the Roman Empire is what motivates Aeneas, but the value of this enterprise too is severely undercut. Aeneas repeatedly abandons promising new beginnings (of which Carthage is the most important and tragic) and engages in numerous harsh actions toward other men and nations, in order to found an empire that will only perpetuate his own involvement in grief and destruction, as the underworld's forecast and his issuance through the gate of false dreams make clear. Consistently, he is figured as a hunter who, in slaying savage but noble beasts, takes on the savagery of his prey.[28] And if Turnus must die to make way for Aeneas, who ruthlessly destroys the culture through which he enters into his kingdom, the Trojans themselves must lose their name and language. The known history of the empire ends with the death of the young Marcellus; the possibility and desirability of world peace based on military prowess are left in doubt.

Dante's poem portrays a hero whose culture has fragmented itself and exiled him; his poem is an explicit lamentation for what was or might have been, and (uniquely among epics) the creation of an ideal Christian community to sustain the poet in his wanderings. The narrator of Ariosto's *Orlando Furioso* does not trouble to conceal his assumptions that the culture's ideals are unworkable and that both love and war are painful and futile.[29] The war solves nothing; afterwards, when Ariosto takes us back to France to see how things are, things are terrible. Institutional religion and even Christianity itself are pilloried. Epic endings are not so much tragic, however, as they are inconclusive: life goes on. Ariosto's jovial tone and marvellous satirical wit make his poem considerably less painful to read than Tasso's, which ends not in triumph at the capture of the city, but in rivers of blood. Tasso's predilection for a "heroism of failure" [30] helps to make his poem fit both distinctively and definitively into the tradition.

In Camoens, there is for the first time an explicit questioning of epic goals. At the harbor where they are to set sail, da Gama's crew are confronted by an old man, who argues that the search for fame wrecks peace, fidelity, and empire, and asks whether they want to be like Prometheus, Phaeton, and Icarus. The explorers do not trouble even to answer him. What for the old man is a rhetorical question to which the obvious answer is "no" would receive a self-evident "yes" from any epic hero. Western heroism is defined that way. "Wretched in truth their lot and strange their nature," Camoens' seafarers will test their own limits because they are who they are, and will thereby at least half-knowingly bring about all the suffering and human degradation that Camoens himself had already seen in the Portuguese empire. More than any previous epic writer in this tradition, Camoens shows a clear awareness of the complexity of human motivation and the near impossibility of doing anything with a pure heart.

Like Ariosto, Spenser did not finish his poem, which in any case would probably be bound to seem as inconclusive as other epics because of its Christian pessimism. But a look at Spenser's explicit use of history suggests a greater degree of perspective than is shown in any previous epic. The history of Britain given Arthur in Book 2 seems to argue for some sort of general human improvement. The same mistakes are not repeated. Every culture eventually destroys itself, but on a level different from those of preceding cultures. Nevertheless, the characters are faced with the same dilemmas that confront other epic heroes: at the end of Book 1, Redcrosse has been given a vision of the heavenly city and denied entrance into it. He must remain in the world, obedient to his destiny, even though his doing so can only involve him in destructive warfare.

Because the *Faerie Queene* is unfinished and Arthur's quest so subordinated to those of the individual knights, it may be best to try to identify within the sixth book Spenser's mature attitude toward goals. There the quest is to trap the Blatant Beast, which is slander, and Calidore, the knight of courtesy, shows very little interest in that undertaking. If previous books of the *Faerie Queene* undo male-female sex roles, this one undoes assumptions about knightly endeavor, since Calidore spends most of his time in a pastoral retreat, and discovers that he can succeed better both in love and in combat without armor than with it. While the Blatant Beast seems to attack people arbitrarily, we learn that its victims can heal their own wounds, and that Arthur is invulnerable to its poison. An avenging knight is needed less than a moral citizenry and the gift of grace. Last of all, we learn that, although Calidore does succeed in his quest, the Blatant Beast has escaped and roams the world again.

The epic hero is asked to live as a flawed man in a flawed world. Even though the poem may purport to celebrate an ideal hero engaged in the founding of an ideal society, as the *Aeneid* does, it also reveals the unattainability of this goal. Each hero has his own individual failings, but the flaw that he shares with others is mortality, symbolized in particular by the opposition between his striving ambition and his varying awareness of the cave and its contents.

The cave is the mind's discovery or invention: since the hero or the poet knows that the unconscious exists, it is already part of the conscious mind. To it are assigned qualities that often produce fear of the self as well as of others—primarily darkness, uncertainty, evil, sexuality, violence. The hero has to keep himself severely under control in order not to be taken over by the cave, and there is a relationship between the extent to which he sees himself obligated to carry out a mission and the severity of the dangers that the cave represents.

Obviously, the hero's mind itself is a cave, and perhaps the more so, the more he has to exercise conscious control over his passions. In these poems, his reaching his goal is often dependent on self-control, although the final episode often demands not only mental alertness but also a great deal of physical force. Thus, a pattern develops in which the hero seems ultimately to discharge himself of an accumulated violence that has been not dispelled but saved up over a long period of time. This is markedly true of Achilles, Odysseus, and Aeneas, who set the pattern for epic heroes to follow, and is particularly apparent in Aeneas, since he has been depicted as the civilized hero in opposition to Turnus. When Aeneas rages at the end of his poem, engaging in unnecessary destruction and slaughter, his behavior calls in question the supposed mission of Rome to bring peace to the world. The raging of Orlando does not come at the end of the *Orlando Furioso*, but rather becomes a symbol of the uncontrolled nature of his whole society. Sometimes violence is made to seem justifiable, as in Odysseus' slaughter of the suitors and Guyon's destruction of the Bower of Bliss, yet there is a fine line between these acts and the excessive violence of Achilles, Aeneas, and the soldiers who pillage Jerusalem. Only Dante, for whom the cave has been so fully objectified, escapes this tendency except for the episodes in which he kicks or otherwise abuses some sinner in Hell, and these are supposed to be examples of courtesy. These poems tell us that it is difficult to react without overreacting, or to hold oneself in control for a long time, as Aeneas does, without building up a reservoir of rage. What is important and difficult, for the reader as well as the character, is to know the range that separates the violent in Dante's Hell from the violence of St. Peter's verbal attack on the popes who usurp his place (*Paradiso*, 27.16–27). Indifference and withdrawal from action are always untenable; one has to take with passion one's given part in the world. But it is hard for anyone ever to know himself entirely, and lack of either self-knowledge or self-possession is often measured in excessive or defective force.

The epic traditionally separates executive from active force, as with Agamemnon and Achilles, or Charlemagne and Orlando: this is partly a comment on the difficulty and the necessity of making those capacities work together. Early in the *Iliad* and in *Orlando Furioso*, the king deprives his chief warrior of a woman, thus bringing about the warrior's defection from battle. It is probably significant that physical strength is coupled with physical desire. A central problem in the *Iliad*, *Orlando Furioso* and *Jerusalem Delivered* is to bring the great force of the chief warrior under useful discipline. Odysseus and Aeneas combine the active and executive forces in themselves, and have to do their own rejecting of temptation.

There are several other characteristic devices for the portrayal of violence. The unruly violent may be devils, pagans, Amazons, or barbarians. These alternatives all permit the violent ones to inhabit their own separate landscapes, far removed from the civilized world, although there is always the threat and usually the reality of conflict brought about by either side. There is also a wild-man theme traditional in western folk-culture,[31] and the wild man or woman does live at least on the edge of society. This figure, who, like Guido Savage in *Orlando Furioso,* or Artegall and Satyrane in the *Faerie Queene,* is often portrayed as half-brother to a hero, is at least a tacit admission that men, who aspire to be gods, share the nature of animals.

The wild-man tradition is extensive and rich. At its edges it might include a person like Clorinda, who was brought up among animals. Or one might think of Spenser's Belphoebe-Amoret pairing, with Belphoebe's extreme intolerance of weakness in love contrasted with Amoret's vulnerability to lust. The wild person, originally pictured as a soulless near-animal, is also seen in the Renaissance as a noble savage uncorrupted by society, and both kinds of wild people inhabit Spenser's poem. The wild person may be seen as having administered law to animals (taming himself), and may have considerable strength of character and even self-discipline, like Spenser's Satyrane or Tasso's Clorinda. As with other portrayals of violence, there is a whole range here from lawless evil to stern justice, as the epic writer tries to accept and work with the idea of man's animal nature.

From the very earliest epics, then, it is apparent that the central theme is not so much heroic enterprise in battle as it is men's struggles with themselves. The *Iliad* is not supposed to be about the Trojan war, but about the wrath of Achilles. The polarities of sex, religion, or civilization depicted in these poems are the polarities and paradoxes of human nature, as is made apparent by the many cross-overs that result in brothers and sisters on opposite sides, warrior women and cowardly men, enemies who are obviously necessary to one another. One of the most signal examples of this is the polarity between Turnus, who is a kind of wild man, and Aeneas, who stands for civilization and order. Before the death of Turnus, Aeneas himself has become violent, and Turnus' death is obviously symbolic; his primitive strength now belongs to Aeneas, who needs it. The new civilization cannot exist without that destructive fiery energy.

The same problem is exemplified in the *Iliad*, where the Trojans, and particularly Hector, represent civilization. Their city is under attack; family life, the stay of civilization, is very much in evidence. Hector fights because of his adherence to accepted codes of behavior—loyalty and honor—not out of any sort of passion or conviction. His choice of code over common sense, in fact, brings about his own and his country's ruin. Achilles in his shelter, living an isolated androgynous life with Patroclus, represents the dark energy of the cave. He fights, finally, with a passion that overwhelms him as well as his adversaries, and that makes him almost incapable of participating in any of the necessary rituals of civilization. The opposition between Hector and Achilles, Aeneas and Turnus, shows the necessity of both control and passion, and their futility. It takes control to build a civilization, but it takes passion to create it; and both contain the seeds of their own destruction.

To be heroic in the epic tradition involves knowing and accepting, and at best learning unsteady control over, the sheer animal energy of human nature. It involves accept-

ing life in a world that does not necessarily improve. And
it requires the acceptance of mortality.

4. *Mortality and Its Evasions*

His heart I know, how variable and vain
Self-left. Least therefore his now bolder hand
Reach also of the Tree of Life, and eat,
And live for ever, dream at least to live
For ever, to remove him I decree
And send him from the Garden forth to Till
The Ground whence he was taken, fitter soile.

[11.92–98]

The genre characteristically demonstrates the necessity
of accepting mortality by (perhaps gratuitously) pointing
out the lack of interesting or possible alternatives. Homer
uses the word "godlike" to describe his heroes, yet the
condition of Homer's gods is intrinsically unheroic, just
because they are born immortal. The life of immortality
is shown to be almost entirely trivial: participating in warfare, gods can be wounded but not killed, and, having
little to do, they fill their lives with petty gossip and
intrigues. The idea of immortality is compelling, and
from the beginning is associated with perfection. Yet the
hero is caught in an eternal paradox: the ideal to which he
aspires not only cannot but must not be attained. There
are occasional glimpses in epic of an idyllic, "godlike,"
and still partly human existence, such as that lived by
Homer's Scherians. But it is not a value judgment to say

there cannot be heroism in an Edenic society; it is merely an aspect of definition. Odysseus would not be himself and could not be heroic if he stayed in Scheria, married to Nausikaa.

Nevertheless, a belief in eternal life does seem to be compatible with heroism. The crucial point is that the hero regards the terms of mortal state as definitive: here his accomplishment must exist. Dante saw his poem as an allegory of the earthly existence of saints and sinners; their condition was what they achieved as mortals. When the Son of God or any other divine being accepts mortal limitations, he can achieve human heroism; when a human escapes his limits simply by evasion, or by fortune (as Odysseus would have if he had stayed with Calypso), he loses that opportunity. The sense of transcendence that some persons experience in ordinary life is redemptive but temporal, not a denial but a fulfillment of mortality. The hero may have such enriching experiences, but he is not permitted within the poem to abandon earthly existence.

Obviously there is a tension here that is analogous to that implicit in the Greek attitude toward immortality. While the Christian is supposed to believe that Heaven is his goal and home, that is a goal he cannot directly seek. If Achilles or Odysseus tried to become immortal, if Redcrosse tried to get to Heaven before his time, even if Vasco da Gama stayed on the Isle of Nymphs, they would all fail to be themselves. It is important that even Dante travels uniquely as one still alive to the realms of the afterlife, so that in some sense he is never really there, and that even so the hardest part of his mission is preserving his consciousness of himself as a verbal human being who must return to describe what he has seen.

The belief in eternal life, just because it provides moments of transcendence, obviously helps to create the dissatisfaction that makes the hero so unwilling to accept his lot, so vulnerable to illicit or unreal alternatives. The concept is not only a part of a religious creed, but an idea, embracing all creeds, of a wholeness like that preceding conscious history. The human search for self-realization and self-transcendence also makes use of the unconscious mind, not in an attempt to get back to the beginning, but both to accept and to transcend the human self-consciousness that has been achieved. This legitimate search, which is a task of epic poetry, will be discussed more fully in the following sections. To the extent that the hero does not or cannot employ all his powers toward this end, the movement forward becomes confused with movement backward toward the beginning that can never be found again, or with efforts to escape or to obliterate conflicts without healing them.

That attempt to get home again is a feature of the *Iliad* that helps to explain the apparent aimlessness of some of its discussions, and of the structure of the poem as a whole. It has been said that the Greek mind at this period is not goal-oriented. Neither Greeks nor Trojans in the poem can imagine the future as well as they can the past. Effectively, there is no world in the *Iliad*, except for the city and the plains of Troy. The beautiful pastoral countryside repeatedly summoned up in epic similes suggests an alternative to the fighting and provides credence for the continual talk among the Greeks of going home. The ships are to be kept in readiness for this possibility. Yet as the poem goes on, the epic similes more and more seem to be only similes, and the talk of leaving is obviously idle.

Home is behind them, forever unattainable, and in some sense they know it.

The backward pull begins to blend with other concepts of escape, of which the most frequently imagined in epic poetry are gardens or garden-worlds, suicide, and madness. Distinct enough in definition, and in some of their manifestations, nevertheless, because they all represent inaction, passivity, and at times oblivion, they do sometimes overlap one another in the poetry. The most frequent and obvious device by which the hero is tempted to forget his mortality is some variation on the enchanted garden.[32] Whether pre-Christian or Christian, this garden is almost always a reminder that you cannot go home again, whether "home" is taken to be as historical as Vergil's Troy, or as psychological as the retreat to a preconscious formless condition. The word "garden" is here used generically, to define a place of timeless enchantment that conflicts with the hero's actual mission. There are no literal gardens in pre-Christian epics, although one might include in this category such places as Little Troy and Scheria. Christian literature, too, contains some non-garden gardens, artificial substitutes for Calypso's cave, the most entertaining being the magic dome by which Ariosto's Atlantes tries to preserve Rogero from mortality.

These gardens are often destroyed, by extraneous forces, or intentionally, by the characters themselves. Meliboe's country is despoiled by brigands, Atlantes' dome by unillusioned Astolpho. Critics have frequently complained of Guyon's Puritan zeal in his destruction of the Bower of Bliss. Such violence, which is apt to seem excessive, is nevertheless in proportion to the complex ambiguous reference of these gardens to the beginnings of the race, the lost homes of the heroes, and the transcendent goals that all seek. The garden may be longed for as ideal, yet knowledge that he is still in mid-journey makes the hero look upon any apparent oasis with mixed feelings, as a shelter from reality. Occasional pastoral idylls do exist, fragile, doomed, and, for the hero, escapist, like Phaeacia and the country of Meliboe. As for the future and transcendent world, the unattainable city of Jerusalem is viewed by St. George from afar. Only Dante is allowed to enter its gardens, and he must leave them behind, half forgetting the reality, in order to use language to describe it. It is good that there is at least once in epic story a record of that process, the near-speechlessness of the attainment set across from the inarticulate formlessness of the original cave.

At its best the garden in epic keeps before the hero a vision of his true purpose, and briefly grants him refreshment and inspiration. At worst, it can menace his humanity, and his existence, as it does in the Bower of Bliss. When it is a snare cast by the forces of darkness, it much resembles man's threatened vision of the original cave, its effects resemble those of suicide and madness, and their near relation to one another shows us why the garden can be so sinister. Most epic heroes consider suicide or fall into madness, especially at crucial times in their lives, when they are being asked to deny what seems dearest to them, to take on an impossible task, and, often simultaneously, to realize that they are only human. Overwhelmed by his own inadequacy, Redcrosse wants to destroy himself rather than run the risk of more mortal behavior. Everyone who reads Book 1 of the *Faerie Queene* notices how emotionally compelling are the arguments of Despair in comparison to the rest of the narrative. This character, who scarcely exists outside his own argument, collects and distills into quintessential debate all conceivable reasons for wanting to die, until he is practically unanswerable.

By acting out a false suicide, Ariosto's Ariodantes gets what he wants, the untainted love of Genevra that he had to begin with. Suicide, or the ritual of it, at best can lead to a new beginning—after all, it has never been clear where suicide leaves off and martyrdom begins. The idea of death to self is compatible with the necessary acceptance of mortality, and Dante is shown as having utterly to resign his old self, to endure a kind of death by fire, in order to achieve Paradise. That effort to achieve a higher consciousness, although different from the suicide that is damnation and the end of everything, resembles it enough to give suicide, like the false garden, a kind of ambiguity. At certain times it is enormously attractive, and so comes to be regarded with both longing and repulsion. In the classical epics, although no particular moral obloquy attaches to suicide, it appears to be something that women do; it is not for the hero to let himself die with Troy. Christianity makes it the worst kind of sin, unending destruction of the self, as Dante shows in his seventh circle. An act of violence itself, but a compelling one, it has to be violently rejected.

Different as they seem, the garden, suicide, and madness all offer chosen oblivion. Maneuvered to Alcina's island by Atlantes, who wishes the safety of his ward above his honor, Rogero equates beauty with goodness and falls under her spell into a life of forgetful ease, far from the confused battles that characterize proper knighthood. Suicide is rejection of the role for which the hero is needed and the unknown perils to which he must expose himself. Madness is a kind of suicide of the mind, protecting Orlando from self-knowledge, and destructive both of himself and of those unfortunate enough to stand in his way. The moon, as Ariosto's repository of lost things, including sanity, signifies the universality of human madness, the difficulty with which self-consciousness is maintained.

Each of these routes involves a kind of crazy hope; otherwise it would not be so compelling. The garden reminds people of Eden or the Golden World. Suicide, phoenixlike, can contain a new beginning. And madness has always figured a higher sanity. In epic tradition such possibilities are minimally realized, but they are there at least to tease and to deceive. Paradise, death to self, the babblings of a soothsayer, all show that the way of negation, rightly held, is a way of life. More predictably, however, the garden, suicide, and madness offer oblivion, an impossible attempt to go back to the original state of unconsciousness. And violence attaches to them, in the attainment of them as goals, in staying with them, and in escaping from them.

Finally rejecting all these alternatives, the hero accepts consciousness, and, eventually, self-consciousness. In order to be heroic, he must be mortal and aware of his mortality; that awareness involves or is involved in the achievement of consciousness. A sense of mortality pervades the mode of tragedy, too, of course, and some epics are tragic.[33] But although the two kinds of heroism may coincide, the emphasis is likely to be quite different. The tragic hero almost always finds that his destiny, that which makes him a hero, and his death are inextricably combined. There is a kind of defiance in his choice of doom. For the epic hero, it is enough simply to accept the fact that he will have to die sometime, and to run the risk of death by choosing his destiny. The way in which his life is played out determines the particular shading the epic receives—comic, tragic, romantic, ironic, or some combination of these. Although I suppose one might call the *Iliad* or the *Aeneid* tragic, because in them death is so pervasive, none of the poems in Milton's tradition is tragic in the way of *Oedipus* or of *King Lear*. At its most extreme, the difference is that between Ishmael and Ahab, Britomart and the Duchess of Malfi, Adam and Hamlet. The epic hero lives to tell his story. He is less terrible and more canny than his tragic counterpart. Believing that life, even with knowledge of death, is important and worthwhile, he commits himself to staying alive and mortal in this world, doing his worldly tasks in the time he is given.

Discovery and acceptance of his own nature and place in life are the role of any human being; the magnitude of his undertaking determines his heroism. Aeneas' helmsman Palinurus is heroic in his refusal to give in to sleep naturally: he fights the god Morpheus until he is knocked overboard with the helm still in hand; his insistence on his duty is what makes him a worthy sacrifice and keeps the ship on course even after his death. Dido and Turnus, blind during life to their fate, finally see and accept what has become of them, and thus gain a measure of heroism at the end. A steadily increasing consciousness marks Dante's progress from Hell to Purgatory and Paradise. Hell's residents are blind, confined in boxes, drowning in lakes; those of Paradise are bounded only by themselves, knowing and fulfilled within their own limits. To be heroic it may be necessary to be larger than other men, but the epic also celebrates these minor characters who are wholly themselves.

But how to become oneself? The desire for intellectual and spiritual experience characterizes the epic hero. Inexperienced Telemachus, at the beginning of the *Odyssey*, is sent out to get news of his father primarily in order to learn something about the world, so that he can become his father's son. Odysseus obviously has spent time getting experience for its own sake. Explaining how Dante, alive, comes to be in Hell, Vergil says that "to give him full experience I, who am dead, must bring him down here" (*Inferno*, 28.48–49). Yet the insatiable desire for experience is also what puts Ulysses into the eighth bolgia of Dante's eighth circle, and it is what makes his story so moving:

> "O brothers," I said, "who through a hundred thousand perils have reached the west, to this so brief vigil of the senses that remains to us choose not to deny experience, in the sun's track, of the unpeopled world. . . . You were not born to live as brutes, but to follow virtue and knowledge." [26.112–20]

The desire for knowledge has its own perils, always. But moral reservations about this quest only emerge with Christianity, when excessive experience begins to seem as dangerous as too little. The very things that give a hero his epic stature make it likely that he will overstep his limits and try to take heaven by storm before he knows his own nature, valuing power and knowledge more than wisdom.

The desire for experience contributes to the conflict, in the tradition, between community and isolation. It has usually been assumed that the hero's values are communal, that he acts not for himself but on behalf of his people. Yet in major episodes of almost every epic the hero is not in his community, but somewhere else. Sometimes, it is true, he has fallen prey to temptation, although even temptation eventually proves instructive. Major spiritual experiences, such as the visit to the underworld, are frequently solitary. The hero wants more than the others do; he pushes back the boundaries of consciousness on their behalf insofar as they represent humanity, but not necessarily *for them* in relation to their immediate interests or well-being. Without Achilles, Odysseus, Rinaldo, or Redcrosse, wars cannot be won and kingdoms saved, but none of them comes to the rescue with all possible speed. They are doing more important and crucial things, without which they could accomplish nothing.

Accomplishment, in fact, is not judged solely, or even primarily, by what we think of as epic action. Action, of some kind, is going to occur, one way or another; what is important is the "fit" between the mind and the action, between the individual and the community. The hero lives both in time and out of it, both in himself and in his given world. Supposedly he rejects senseless isolation for purposeful community, although often community is only valuable as an end in itself and not for the common cause that holds it together. In the *Iliad* men knowingly and enduringly join in an unjust war. Hector, who dislikes fighting as much as anyone, regrets that he must die, because he will not have time to teach his son to carry a spear. The shield of Aeneas enables him to carry on his shoulders the fortunes of the race. To some extent, community atones for mortality. If a man cannot live forever, perhaps mankind can, and participation even in the bloodiest warfare can then assure an individual's place in human history.

On the other hand, the hero is given considerable reason to question the merit and even the existence of historical continuity, especially on any level that can be personally meaningful to him. Achilles is strikingly isolated from his companions; almost no appeals to family or tribal loyalty can touch him. Throughout his poem, Aeneas is systematically deprived of almost everyone who has been important to him. Dante the character is soon to go into perpetual exile. The exaggeratedly episodic, fragmentary organization of *Orlando Furioso* is intended to demonstrate life's incoherence, the difficulty of achieving and maintaining any central purpose. The personal lives of these people are always at odds with their lives as soldiers, and matter to them much more than the battle of Paris does. Yet, badly or well, sooner or later the hero comes back and does what he has to do.

He is isolated from others by his superior skills, by his destiny, and by his knowledge. He is a target for others' envy, even when his position is to him unenviable. Who would choose to be Achilles or Rinaldo? He is asked, at a moment's notice, to end relationships that have meant much, as Aeneas must, or to learn, like Dante, that an old friend and guide is condemned to eternal pain in the Inferno. He is isolated by the fact that he is in progress and cannot attach himself to any community along the way or confuse his needs with theirs. Sometimes he can tell his destination only negatively: this is not it.

It is often difficult for the reader to like him, since the hero's needs require him to seem inhuman at times.

Odysseus uses his men as bait; Dante kicks a former acquaintance in the face; the parting of Aeneas and Dido is notorious. It is ordinarily impossible for the hero to cultivate kindness or generosity; although he is capable of these, he must also be prepared to turn away from all human bonds. But even if he seems at times to be denying the immediate for the sake of the remote, and the personal for the theoretical, that is not the whole story either. Many of the great moments of epic occur when an immediate rush of feeling takes on inevitability: it is countenanced or even required in the scheme of things, and personal and abstract come together. The point is that the hero must be open to everything, not closed in by his own limitations and personal expectations or commitments.

Both meetings and partings in epic tend to have this kind of wonderful inevitability because they are especially likely to involve mission, historical necessity, heavenly decree. The characters themselves are aware of the rightness of what is happening to them, and, when it is pleasurable, the pleasure is thus made particularly intense. The meeting of Britomart and Artegall is such a necessary and yet spontaneous moment; others are the meetings of Dante and Vergil, and Dante and Beatrice. Turnus bitterly accepts his death as right and so underlines for us the whole course of his life in the poem as right and even as heroic. On the other hand, the best of Hector's life as hero is recognized and embraced by him at a moment when he joyfully recognizes his military prowess and wishes that the gods would always so bless him.

Epic describes the process in which human beings are involved, and, within that process, their relationships to themselves, each other, and their goals. The specified goals are likely to be remote, unsatisfactory, or even unattainable. Their relationships are undependable, and almost arbitrarily denied. There exists only a human community, held together by a temporal purpose that may never be realized, by its common humanity, and by a seldom expressed but ever-present longing for a wholeness that can somehow transcend the mortal state. The hero has to be free of definition, and at the same time submissive to needs that the community itself may not know it has. Dante's community (aside from the heavenly city) is an Italy that he himself created.

While the epic characters always change the world in which they live, they also in some way accept it, not necessarily ideologically but existentially. They do not always either believe or disbelieve in the common cause, but they have no way of creating a different context except by living out their extended awareness within their given world. They are called, and they choose to be what they are, and by choosing create their freedom. Their acceptance of themselves makes possible the "tragic joy" so strongly felt in Homer's poems, the love of sensuous detail, even of the instruments of warfare, the joyous capacity to eat, sleep, or make love in the intervals between battles. Ariosto's robust cynicism has the same impetus: nothing matters, in a way, and human beings are all lost; yet their existential capacity for freedom is endless, and is exceeded only by the reader's (and the writer's) enjoyment of the human spectacle.

What matters is the individual's fulfillment within the terms he is given; the terms themselves cannot be changed. Hector has to teach his son to throw a spear if he wants the boy to grow up; Achilles has to rejoin the war if he wants a place among men. That is, one has to accept death if he wants to live. But if that means that one has to live in history, it also means that recognition of history, and mortality, makes one free. History—a perceived pattern of sequential action—is the form that western man has chosen for human existence. Yet objective acknowledgment of that form—seeing it for what it is—is freedom from it. Because history is permeated with mortality, it cannot hold anyone's entire loyalty or existence.

The epic hero, then, is a person with godlike longings or capabilities, who must paradoxically accept his limitations and his limited context in order to be heroic. He is aware of his need to fulfill himself in a limited place and time, even though he may not entirely understand or believe in his given mission. He confronts in himself the caves and dark woods that have always been human symbols of formlessness, ignorance, and unconsciousness, and often of darkness, sexuality, evil, and danger. He is aware of, and prey to, violence, even though (or perhaps because) he may be the most conscious, controlled man of his time. Because of his self-awareness and his commitment to particular goals, he is vulnerable to calls from the opposite extreme—to indulge in sensual delight, to die, to retreat into madness. He is always won back to the community and group endeavor, even though he often has no particular commitment to them. He participates uneasily in human affairs, rejecting any ties that would require him to ally himself permanently with something finished; he is in process. In some way, he works for and represents his people, but the value of his or their goal is uncertain and his movements as portrayed in the poem may seem destructive. He forces a way for people to a new dimension of awareness. He belongs to a community committed to history and freed from history by death, learning the way out of time by awareness of time.

5. *Separation and the Search for Transcendence*

> But Man by number is to manifest
> His single imperfection, and beget
> Like of his like, his Image multipli'd,
> In unitie defective, which requires
> Collateral love, and deerest amitie.
>
> [8.422–26]

The achievement, use, and transcendence of self-consciousness is not only definitive of epic; it is a central characteristic of western art, directly related to the myth of the fall. Perhaps all myths of Paradise refer to the earliest stage of human development, when there is no division into conscious and unconscious worlds, and no loneliness because no sense of self. With self-consciousness come suffering, the knowledge of separateness, and a sense of loss and guilt. The formation of self proceeds by recognition of negatives (I am not that) and opposites. We have seen how this process seems to involve an association of the unconscious mind with passions and desires that can annihilate the self if insufficiently controlled. The traditional prescription for this human condition is to find the virtues of its defects, acquiring a fuller kind of awareness that, as Milton would have it, can by means of education "repair the ruins of our first Parents." The story of every epic is that of the hero allowing himself to accept definition as a mortal being, exposing himself to all the knowledge and dangers and suffering that humanity brings, and then learning to transcend his own definition. Epic also invites the reader to self-discovery, not only by means of the hero's story, but in the form of the poem itself, which by nature and genealogy is what it teaches.

The wholeness toward which an epic education leads the hero is as far beyond discursive reason as the original wholeness is below it. As that original state has so often been associated with danger and evil, it is particularly needful to have a symbol or symbols for positive satisfactions that also have to be associated with the unconscious mind because they are not entirely accessible to ordinary awareness. The most familiar embracing symbol for this condition is of course Heaven, but it is also familiar as an earthly state of transcendental awareness. The means by which the hero is specifically prepared to reach this kind of fulfillment are all interwoven with the earthly experiences by which he reconciles himself with his mortality. His quest is a paradox, for unless he accepts the fact that he is mortal, he cannot learn to transcend himself. He acquires both self-knowledge and self-transcendence through a wide variety of reflecting images. He is educated in self and in otherness by seeing himself, his twin, his opposite, his false self, his other half, or, finally, his whole transcendental being brought near to him in art, and in many different kinds of encounters with other people. Passing beyond mortal comprehension as it does, this education is dangerous: evil adheres to it, and deceits which play upon ordinary understanding. The stubborn self-defining intelligence that raised the mind above the level of the cave is still needed, but it is inadequate defense against deceptions that depend on human reason for their effectiveness. To pass beyond illusion the hero must have recourse to the very unconscious forces which he had to surpass in order to become heroic. If this requires self-abandonment, that does not mean self-loss, but rather a gradual erasing of the limits of consciousness on the boundary between self and other.

Epics are full of episodes containing art within art, in which the contained art reflects or interprets the larger meaning. Beginning with Achilles, the characters sing their own exploits. They find their deeds recorded in many kinds of art—Juno's shrine in Carthage; the pictures on shields; the tapestry into which Helen weaves the story of Troy; the funeral games of the Trojans at the death of Anchises. Rinaldo is made to confront his own image in an adamantine shield; the history of Portuguese deeds is portrayed in banners on their flagship; Britomart and Arthur read their own histories. The technique functions first of all to create, restore, or increase self-consciousness, enabling people to see themselves as others do and describe themselves as they would like to be seen.

Epic teaches us that art as we know it requires the acceptance or experience of mortality. It needs that kind of definition and boundaries. That is the lesson we learn when, for example, Odysseus, after renouncing immortality with Calypso, is able to sing his own adventures and hear them sung. On Calypso's island, he was almost indefinable apart from her—a shadowy, tearful, impotent figure. In Scheria, he stands out in clear relief, as a very mortal and temporary visitor. Tears accompany his effort to break from Calypso into consciousness, and they accompany art in the epic as well: he weeps in Scheria when his tale is told. Looking at the story of Troy on the walls of Juno's shrine, Aeneas exclaims, "There are tears for passing thing; here, too, things mortal touch the mind" (1.462). The art of the funeral game is directly inspired by death, distancing mortality by playing at it.

Art is a way to achieve immortality in worldly terms, since it outlives its authors. It has also frequently been used as a moral instrument. In Dante's *Purgatorio*, the penitent are constantly made more fully aware of their condition by means of quotations, pictures, dream-visions, and songs inciting them to a better life, in which they themselves will become art. Characters asked to read their own histories are given scripts by which to live. And patrons to whom the poems are dedicated are being asked to know themselves better. Queen Elizabeth, "mirrour of grace and majestie divine" (proem, stanza 4), is shown many other mirrors of herself in the *Faerie Queene*, some more favorable than others. The proems show that she is the inspiration, the content, and the intended pupil of the epic.[34]

Art can create distance, necessary for self-awareness. Also necessary for self-awareness is the splitting off of opposites from unity, the creation of heaven and earth, day and night, subject and object, male and female, good and evil, innocence and guilt, "I" and "you." As consciousness increases, so does human isolation, but the isolation makes possible relatedness, the means by which divisions (which made self-consciousness possible) are to be healed. Self-consciousness is its own disease and its own cure.

At every stage a mistaken kind of self-love is easy. Because it is better than self-hatred, it seems desirable, and there is a feeling of wholeness about it too. Self-consciousness is often described as the ability to see oneself as in a mirror, distinct. But the myth of Narcissus shows the danger: in love with himself, he is lost in his own image. Looking into Armida's eyes, Rinaldo sees her and falls into a state of static enchantment; looking into his eyes, she sees herself: the narcissistic person ruins herself and those around her. Others mirror us; we mirror ourselves. Without such help, there is no self-knowledge. The problem with human relationships is identical to that of man's desire to be godlike. Homer's gods are less godlike than his heroes. Self-knowledge cannot exist without relationships, which cannot exist without separation. The difficulty is to overcome the separation without being annihilated.

Epics are full of pairings, mirrorings, coincidence of opposites, all of which bewilder, instruct, deceive, destroy, and save. A standard kind of relationship is provided by the convention of guest-friendship, which ranges from simple entertainment to a very complex mutuality. Almost never is it only a means to help the traveler on his way. Rather, the ways in which host and guest reflect and illuminate one another's experience can be decisive in their lives. They study one another or involve themselves with one another with a peculiar intensity. In these often-dangerous encounters, self-knowledge is acquired, tested, or rejected by either guest or host or both.

The pattern of questing or journeying that is basic to epic narrative makes visits a natural and even necessary device. And the infrequency of journeying in earlier times makes such visitations inevitably more significant than they now could be. Often it is unknown in advance whether the place and person to be visited are friendly or hostile; in the same manner, the host is often ignorant of his visitor. Yet conventions of hospitality in a world that is hard to travel require that the effort of guest-friendship be made. It is necessarily filled with the ambiguous tension of guarded interest: in this initial attitude, host and guest already mirror one another. Prosperous Dido and shipwrecked Aeneas have a classical sort of guest-friendship—wary at first, they become increasingly friendly as they see how much they have in common, her own flight from an old life running parallel to his. As they grow together, however, she begins to lose her place as founder of a new realm, and he plays at ruling until he is recalled to his own quest, which leads to her immediate ruin and the eventual ruin of Carthage itself.

Odysseus in all his travels is dependent on guest-friendships for enlightenment; because of his somewhat ruthless cleverness, the friendship is usually more beneficial to him than to those visited, who, like the Scherians, run the risk of destruction for their pains. Odysseus repeatedly conceals or plays with his identity in new situations, testing both himself and his hosts. When his father is on the way home, Telemachus, who claims to know nothing of himself, goes visiting, paralleling in a small way his father's experience, and learning enough of himself to become worthy of his father. Dante is a guest in

Hell (though often an unwanted one), in Purgatory, and in Paradise, learning much about his human nature from the souls he visits. In the House of Temperance, Arthur and Guyon are both attended by women who reflect dominant characteristics in their own natures: as Alma says to Guyon,

> Why wonder yee
> Faire Sir at that which ye so much embrace?
> She is the fountaine of your modestee;
> You shamefast are, but *Shamefastnesse* it selfe is shee.
>
> [2.9.43]

Both Arthur and Guyon have at first been taken aback by the demeanor of these women, and need to have their likenesses explained. Then they come to be more at home with their own natures.

It is not by accident that Arthur and Guyon thus learn themselves by looking at women. The roles of women in epic poetry are significant and archetypal, as, to some extent, we have already seen. Obviously, a major separation that consciousness brings about is that between male and female: the mythic first parent is hermaphroditic, and there is a tradition that Adam was hermaphroditic before the creation of Eve. There are significant role divisions between men and women in epic, although these are not inevitable, and they change considerably through the centuries. In general, the male hero is a clearly defined, recognizably human and mortal person who moves through time and space to perform a specific action or task. Many of the major female characters are less clearly defined, are much less often described in action, and have no specific quest. They are often identified with a particular place which, however, their spheres of influence may transcend.

Obviously the male-female polarity is of much more importance than most other kinds of oppositions in the epic because it is so inclusive and so basic. I have said before that the female symbol is not necessarily to be identified with real women, but is involved with a whole complex of things—night, space, eternity, intuition, sensuousness, receptivity, experience—which are traditionally associated with one another, and opposed to maleness, day, time, intellect, activity, argument.[35] The epic works out in terms of characters the problems posed by these sometimes self-defeating oppositions. Because so much can be symbolized in relationships between men and women, the male-female polarity comes to stand for a great deal.

Most of the women in epics can be classified into one or more of the following categories: (1) the cave and its attendant associations with unconsciousness, darkness, the unknown, mystery, evil; (2) relatives and helpmates, mothers or sisters; (3) the cause or way of human activity and its reward. The magnitude of all these female figures —the fact that they so much transcend ordinary human boundaries—is not so much a comment on men's idea of women as it is on the human character's sense of limitedness. While it would seem that the division ought to be described in terms of more equality, the consciousness describing it is always male and naturally tends to associate all the unknown, mysterious forces of the universe with something totally different from himself. He does imagine some sort of supreme force which is male, like him, but that force is detached and remote, like Zeus, or else is a predecessor whose powers are limited like his own. The hero's task is generally to free himself or stay free from the women associated with darkness, to stay in alliance with the women who act as mothers or sisters, and to achieve unity with those who are both way or cause and goal.

The shelter that is Achilles' cave is shared not with a woman but with Patroclus, that androgynous figure who is like Achilles' other self, so close that Achilles can scarcely survive without him. This is psychologically as well as literally the earliest rendition of the cave among these epics, before the male character becomes fully aware of his difference from all that surrounds him. Odysseus has Calypso, who is less threatening than monotonous: she is different from him in being female and immortal, but she is dangerous only in her desire to keep him from re-entering the world, escaping the womb. Elsewhere, however, women are frequently associated with danger. They are witches or witchlike: they can hold men powerless, turn them to animals, drive them mad, or kill them. At the beginning, none of these figures can much influence a hero outside of her own place; Circe, the Sirens, the women associated with Turnus do not journey. Later witch-women include Alcina, Armida, Duessa, Lucifera, and Acrasia. Some, like Lucifera, are still entirely identified with their own residences; others, like Armida, can travel as much as the hero himself. That, I suppose, is an incipient recognition that one is always vulnerable to the dark places of the mind.

Most of these figures lack independent personalities, and are identifiable primarily by the apparatus with which they work their wiles. In Homer, who is not judgmental,

they have real sexual charm. In most of the later epics,
the poet reveals that charm to be bogus, a façade masking
underlying evil. Thus, while Odysseus can have sexual
relations with Circe because he is a match for her (which
his men are not), in Christian epics such dalliance is always dangerous. Yet it also seems necessary. All these
characters test the hero's power to withstand sensual temptation and its accompanying oblivion. To give in to them
is at best to fall back to a prehuman state. But their power
is so great that unless the hero confronts it and learns consciously to detach himself from it, he is always vulnerable. And there are plenty of examples of characters who
cannot learn, who even choose not to learn, like Elpenor,
who drunkenly falls off Circe's roof, or Gryll, who would
rather be Acrasia's hog than a man.

Almost the only thing to be done with these figures is
to subdue or escape them, although there are hints at
more. Odysseus was Circe's lover, and Rinaldo chooses to
be the captive Armida's knight. Since the enchantresses do
not get killed, they have to be continuously acknowledged.
Odysseus and Circe, in a guiltless world, can take delight
in each other's powers. But Armida has to abandon her
magic, and although Rinaldo says he will be her knight,
he has more life-and-death power over her than she ever
had over him. She has been subdued, the price she pays
for becoming human.

Except for Armida, witch-women are less female characters than they are symbols of the cave. Women warriors in epic are real people, but they also acknowledge
men's combined fear of and fascination with what seems
utterly alien and mysterious. Like the witch-women, they
are symbols of the past, not of human beginnings, but of a

matriarchal stage of civilization. In almost every epic, and generally on the wrong side, they are nevertheless almost always treated as admirable. Spenser's negative portrait of Radigund is exceptional in the tradition. But the idea of the woman who dares to "war with men" (*Aeneid*, 1.493) is obviously both fascinating and frightening. Reports of Amazons who form their own female society, and admit men only in order to use them, persist in travelers' tales through the Renaissance.[36] The men who kept the records and wrote the epics did not have to commemorate women in this way, and fear of such a society might have more prudently dictated its elimination from human consciousness, or at least the portrayal of such women in less favorable terms. There is fear. But as the epic witnesses to the universal male-female polarity, it also suggests the possibility of a world in which women can flourish as well as men.

Tasso, Spenser, and Ariosto in particular make quite explicit the ambiguity of the tradition. Tancred kills and then baptizes Clorinda, whom he loves. Both Ariosto and Spenser present a variety of valiant women, ranging from two heroines as worthy as any men—Bradamante and Britomart—to Radigund the cruel Amazon queen, and this would seem equivalent to their treatment of men. But their authorial comments appear self-contradictory. Although Spenser's whole poem celebrates the Faerie Queene and frequently pauses to praise famous women, he also seems to undercut himself by taking time out to denounce female rule. In his poem Belphoebe rescues her weaker sister from the tyrant who exemplifies lust, and Britomart has to rescue Artegall, her lover, from the Amazon Radigund, who has put him in women's clothes.

Tyranny makes any relationship impossible, he seems to be saying: cold-hearted Belphoebe causes pain without knowing it, but equality in love can accommodate equality in strength.

Women appear also in more ordinary roles, as mothers and companions. More mobile and limited than the witches and less gifted as mortal beings than the Amazons, they are to some extent in bondage to mortality, even though they may be goddesses. Mothers have given birth to mortal men; sisters and lovers care greatly about their men and may be mortal themselves. The most significant mothers are in two of the earliest epics—Thetis, mother of Achilles, and Venus, mother of Aeneas; they do little except to demonstrate the pain of a mixed loyalty, and to remind us of their sons' heritage. More complex relationships are the companionate ones, which may be or become sexual. Examples of these are Odysseus and Athena, Redcrosse and Una. Odysseus and Athena are real mirror images, who enjoy themselves in one another. Una and Redcrosse, on the other hand, are distinct enough to work sometimes athwart each other, sometimes to one another's benefit. Athena can safely leave Odysseus alone much of the time, because her strengths are his: she knows what he can do. Separated, Una and Redcrosse cannot achieve their objective, which requires their combined powers. Both pairs enhance, correct, and enable one another.

The most comprehensive relationships of all, and the most difficult to describe, are those in which women function as either cause or way, and as end. Such women are the direct opposite of Calypso, who stands for the mysterious darkness from which men have emerged: they are the mysterious light toward which men go and in which at best they travel. As the emergence from original darkness is painful because it involves so much separation and knowledge of death, the movement toward these women can often happily involve the restoration of wholeness on a higher level. Consciousness is an instrument of progress, yet the end is a mystery, beyond logic.

Two transitional figures are Helen and Angelica, both beautiful, dangerous, and irresistible. Helen is cause and goal of the Trojan war, and a mystery even to herself. The old Trojan men who speak of her unearthly beauty testify to the inevitability of wars being fought for her, yet the logic is nonexistent. She does not even comprehend herself, or sense that her life is real. Angelica, too, often seems more symbol than reality. Her loveliness draws all men to her, yet her constant vanishing and reappearing, not always at her own pleasure, makes her unapproachable by them, and makes the reader wonder whether she exists. It is her fate finally to love Medoro, who is more virtuous than Paris, but otherwise no more deserving of her than Paris is of Helen. Helen and Angelica do not choose to be dangerous: unlike the witches, they too are at the mercy of the world, and their own beauty deprives them of stability.

Penelope and Beatrice are more fulfilled and fulfilling characters. Penelope is as wily as her husband, maintaining her freedom in such a way that, whatever happens, she will survive. That is important in itself: she and Odysseus are mutual mirrors, deserving of one another.[37] Odysseus does not exactly hurry home from the war. True, he is at the mercy of various unfriendly forces. But he unnecessarily explores some places, like the domains of Circe and the Cyclops. He is unquenchably thirsty for experience. Penelope makes it possible for time to stand still while he learns. Homer is not a time-conscious poet to begin with, of course. But the passage of time is marked in the poem by frequent mention of how long Odysseus has been gone, by the growing up of Telemachus, and by the increasing impatience and impudence of the suitors. Yet Telemachus, though a man in years, has not matured; the suitors have been maintained like tame geese; time has not critically affected Odysseus' kingdom. Penelope's weaving and unweaving of her web also connects her with both the fates and eternity.[38] She controls events, controls time. And her weaving connects her with the ancient female symbol of the spider, gathering in and immobilizing the suitors, but also at long range gathering in Odysseus himself. The poem makes the reader feel her power all the time, bringing her husband home.

Again there is identification of woman with place. Helen is in the wrong place, and her location in Troy marks that city for seige and destruction. Dido is identified with her city and its fate. On Ithaca, Penelope is a match for the invaders, as she is for Odysseus, who has to invade his own domain. Once Odysseus recaptures Ithaca, he intends to leave again, as St. George does, when Una is re-established in her kingdom. Yet obviously this does not simply mean that male is active and female passive. Una, after all, goes to get St. George, and makes it possible for him to become who he is when he arrives at her Eden. Both Redcrosse and Dante are hopelessly incompetent at the beginning of their poems to handle their own lives. Redcrosse does not even have an identity; Dante defines himself in negatives—he is not Aeneas or St. Paul. Both learn self-mastery only through the guidance of their women. Beatrice leaves her footprints in Hell for Dante, to insure that he can become himself and thereby an inheritor of the heavenly city.

In the beginning the mysteriousness of the woman was a sign of the unknown origins of consciousness. Then it became a threat. Now it can signify the regaining of wholeness, mysterious because wholeness cannot be fully comprehended. The woman gathers in; the man wanders. Sometimes, as with Beatrice and Gloriana, she is there at the beginning and at the end, sending forth and receiving again. Her wholeness means that she does not have to wander; all things come to her or are contained in her, although she may sometimes have to leave her place to bring someone to her. Sometimes man's resentment or fear of her power is her destruction: she is seen as threat, like Dido in Carthage, Clorinda in Jerusalem. Penelope and Una are strong enough to resist threat and find deliverance. The city of Beatrice is beyond all possibility of threat, a city that will gather in its citizens until it contains all.

Although, as I have said before, antithetical female-male imagery is symbolic, not literal, such symbolism obviously is taken literally in sex characterization through these epics. Even in Spenser, who builds and improves upon romance tradition in employing major female heroines who function like male heroes in the world, Britomart's primary task is to find Artegall, her mate. Nevertheless, both she and Ariosto's Bradamante are their own women, unmysterious, with clearly individualized motivation. The freeing of women from typical roles accompanies the man's freeing of himself from fears which he had located in her. Bradamante is a woman living in history, opposing her sure knowledge of Ruggiero's destiny to the fantastic efforts of Atlantes to save his ward from mortal life. Britomart is described as combining in herself manly terror with amiable grace. Artegall, in learning to become worthy of her, goes from one extreme to the other, first depending on the strong man Talus, then allowing himself to be taken captive by the beauty of the Amazon Radigund. Spenser's characters are learning to acknowledge and integrate the opposite poles of being within themselves.

So far I have discussed two ways by which the epic hero can learn and test his identity in relation to others. He can simply acknowledge his difference from and his need for other people. That is what the convention of guest-friendship does. When Agamemnon came home from the war, he was unprepared for his reception by Aegisthus and Clytemnestra: he had been replaced in his absence, and could be neither guest, friend, nor husband in his own house. That is why Odysseus' extreme caution seems so necessary, not only in testing matters in Ithaca, but in his whole way of choosing and asserting his identity all the way home. The second means of learning and testing is through relationships with women and, more generally, one's own unconscious mind. If the hero has succeeded well enough in defining himself, separating himself from nothingness and the dangers of nothingness (the Cyclops, Calypso), then Penelope, not Clytemnestra, will be waiting for him at the end. His own opposite qualities are restored to him as treasure, not destruction, and he becomes whole.

Throughout epic it is apparent that no choices are simple: the hero cannot often establish a relationship with either a person or a place based on the evidence that he thinks his senses give him. Sensory pleasures are seldom rejected by the epic hero; temperance is called for, but the world is to be enjoyed. Nevertheless, the senses cannot be trusted for critical decisions. Milton in *Areopagitica* argues that good and evil are almost indistinguishable from one another, and even in Homer's poems, where moral judgments are less frequent than they are later, look-alikes constantly deceive. The use of twins, doubles, and other ocular deceptions is very old in literature, and obviously accompanies the struggle to achieve and surpass consciousness and self-consciousness.

The mind plays upon itself the tricks that it wants to play. Hector, deceived to his death by the false Deiphobus outside the gates of Troy, fought the war because he believed in comradeship. Dido and Aeneas need to fall in love with each other: their lives are look-alikes, and their need is facilitated by Cupid masked as Ascanius. The trick is worked from outside because, especially in these early poems, consciousness is externalized. Later, it is still done that way, but the hero's responsibility for his decisions becomes more obvious, and the gods are less likely to be involved. In Ariosto's poem, the magician Atlantes proliferates look-alikes in order to keep Ruggiero captive, and even though Bradamante has been told that she will have to kill a phantom copy of her lover, she cannot bring herself to do it. Tasso uses the same device in his dark wood, to keep the heroes from their task. Redcrosse Knight, with his defective vision, cannot distinguish between Una and Duessa, and the false Florimel seems to all the world to be real.

So, relationships are essential to self-knowledge and

self-fulfillment, but the world is made in such a way that establishment and maintenance of these relationships seem almost impossible to achieve. The senses bring enjoyment of the world, but they can never be trusted, as we see again and again in the false gardens of Alcina, Armida, Acrasia. Guyon, whose story is temperance, so intemperately destroys the Bower of Bliss because its pleasures really lead to a stupefaction of the senses. The many unmaskings of false bowers and maidens show that, again and again, their overwrought devices deceive people into making love to what is rotten and corrupt, thereby becoming less human rather than more so. And so, as one must learn to detach oneself from a part of one's own mind (the unconscious) in order to possess it, one must learn detachment from the senses in order to enjoy them accurately. Sense knowledge tells Odysseus that Calypso and Nausikaa are more beautiful than Penelope, but his whole being tells him that Penelope is more important: knowing that, he can enjoy Calypso and Nausikaa without being absorbed by them.

The problem is seldom that obvious, however. Not even being told the plain truth saves Ariosto's characters, but the magic ring of Angelica, which is identified with reason, does (8.2). This ring not only reveals everything else as it is; it also makes the wearer invisible, and therefore usually free from danger. The aspect of invisibility is interesting. It removes the wearer from the sense knowledge of others, but possibly it also suggests that removal from one's own senses (the temporary disappearance of the body) may have some relation to right judgment. Although the ring is identified with reason, it is obvious that reason, which after all is at least partly based on sensory evidence, is not enough. It is reasonable of the Redcrosse Knight to suspect Una of infidelity when (as far as he can see) he catches her in the act. It is reasonable of Hector to think that Deiphobus is helping him. But the mind and the body are so interrelated, and so flawed, that judgments made in the body cannot be depended on. Ariosto's tone is comic, and his means of releasing characters from their bodies is temporary and illusory; yet the device is not altogether different from the more serious ordeal of Dante, who has to pass through fire, purging himself from lust and the last weakness of the senses, in order truly to become master of himself.

It is wholly unreasonable, it would seem, to depend for clarity on magic rings and purging flames. I have said that Penelope was waiting for Odysseus because he succeeded in self-definition, and it is true that Odysseus considers all aspects of every problem that he encounters. But he does not always use reason, and if he had been married to Clytemnestra, not Penelope, everything might have come out differently. Penelope is his way as well as his reward, and it is something other or more than reason that saves the heroes. Reason is not enough, any more than the conscious mind is enough. One becomes conscious in order to transcend consciousness, and rational in order to reach beyond reason. The necessity for a fuller kind of consciousness is very well shown in the treatment of women already described. The women of epic poems who are associated with origin and end can almost be said to create their men. Thus, in the *Faerie Queene*, Britomart, who has seen Artegall only in a magic glass, is more overjoyed to hear him praised than a mother is, after carrying a child for nine months, to see it emerge safely (3.2.11). Beatrice's eyes are repeatedly described as mirrors through which Dante receives illumination.

Mirroring connects the woman outside with the self within. Obviously, looking at oneself in a mirror is dangerous: that is the Narcissus story. But if the image of God in man is the soul, then contemplation of oneself is a valid religious activity: one of Dante's dreams in Purgatory shows him Rachel, sitting all day before her mirror, enamoured of her own eyes (*Purgatorio*, 27.94–108). And mirrors are repeatedly used for self-education in epics, as we have already seen in such devices as the mirroring shields. The walls of Logistilla's palace, to which Ariosto's Ruggiero repairs after his stay with Alcina, are made of a material that reflects men's bodies and souls:

> Looking at himself in the bright mirroring surfaces, he sees himself truly, knows himself, and grows wiser; he will not fall for false praise or false blame, either. Moreover, the clear light of this stone imitates the sun, shining so brightly that whoever has such stone, wherever he is, can make daylight whenever he wants. . . . [p. 155]

The brightness of self-knowledge that in Dante makes the body luminous seems to emphasize the connection between self-knowledge and relationships with others. The souls in Purgatory and Paradise begin to intuit one another; thoughts are reflected back and forth like light:

> "Pray, bring to my wish speedy fulfillment, blest spirit," I said, "and give me proof that what I think I can reflect on thee." [*Paradiso*, 9.18–20]

> "I would not await thy question if I were in thee as thou art in me." [*Paradiso*, 9.80–81]

The lives of St. Thomas and St. Francis (founders of opposing orders) are made to describe and praise one another, and the Cross of Souls "flames forth Christ" (14.104). Intuitive reasoning of the sort possessed by angels has brought these souls to unity with one another and with Christ. Contemplation of self has become identical with wholeness.

The fact that the epic aims at psychic integrity is the reason why its scale has to be cosmic. Whatever opposite poles sky and earth may represent, there is always a relationship between the macrocosm and the human microcosm: the hero learns to reach out toward and to include the whole range of being. And he has to acknowledge information received from these sources. Every epic has at least one heavenly messenger,[39] and either a visit to or messages from the underworld. From these sources the hero learns what he cannot learn by human reason.

Every epic contains prophecy. The hero's mind is not only coextensive with his world; it also includes the past and the future. From books, visions, dreams, lectures, visits, he learns the story of his people and his own place in it. The prophecy is not always clear to us: scholars have never come to agreement about the meaning of what Aeneas learns in the underworld. But clarity is not its function; prophecy is intrinsically an affront to the analytic human mind. As sky and underworld extend the hero in space, prophecy extends his command of time, and by these means he becomes godlike.

A more familiar kind of transcendence in time is achieved through the bond between fathers and sons, and in this group are spiritual as well as biological fathers. One of

Achilles' important characteristics (negative as it is) is his lack of a father, the sense he has of being unrelated, in this context of warfare, to what is happening. He constantly longs to go home, recover his own son, and lead a life that makes sense to him. One of Priam's important characteristics is that he is so much a father. The sense of family life, and the tragedy of its disruption, is what distinguishes the city of Troy from the Greek camp outside. At the end, the search for his son Hector is what brings Priam to Achilles. They remind one another explicitly of the importance of relationships between fathers and sons, and as they look at one another are reminded both of the wonder and of the suffering of humanity. In each other's presence they are able to sleep and eat again, reaffirming in one another the continuity of life.

Aeneas cannot leave his father in Troy, as Anchises desires, because he is necessary to the first part of the enterprise. In the structure of his poem, Vergil demonstrates the epic's concern with the mysterious relationship between past and future. Anchises can lead Aeneas to his own limits, but for both of them the pull backward to their known, lost lives is almost overwhelming. In settlements like Little Troy, it becomes apparent both how hard it is to forget the past, and how dangerous it is to dwell in it. Anchises' death is part of the pattern of loss in the first six books that forces Aeneas out on his own. When Anchises dies, his son begins to be called Father Aeneas. But only the knowledge of Anchises from beyond life's limits really enables Aeneas to turn toward the future, though that knowledge is burdensome in its obscurity as well as in its importance.

Aeneas' search for his father has been a search for his

new self; making a final visit to the past, he discovers the future. Telemachus has a similar, though less weighty experience. Ignorant of himself and his father (near the beginning of the *Odyssey*, he says that he does not know himself to be Odysseus' son), he goes looking for himself in seeking news of Odysseus. In this poem, there is no involvement with history. Telemachus and Odysseus simply affirm one another's present; they have made themselves worthy of each other.

Hero of his own poem, Dante takes Vergil as his father and guide through the first part of his journey. Both Dante and Statius, another poet whom the two meet in Purgatory, have made Vergil their model, yet they cannot end where Vergil did. Their relationships are properly more Vergilian than Homeric. Vergil showed Statius the way to Christianity without finding it himself; he takes Dante to Paradise without being able to get there himself; his last action in the poem is to crown and mitre Dante as his own sovereign. Still more guides emerge in Paradise, to illumine and also to test. Peter, James, and John examine Dante on faith, hope, and love, respectively. Bernard of Clairvaux gives him his last instruction in contemplative wisdom.

The idea of the father as mirror and guide ought to flourish under Christianity, as it does very clearly in Dante. It does so, but its mode changes, becoming more tentative as it is crowded out of or confused by romance, and by the competition between classical and Christian motifs. In Ariosto, Tasso, and Spenser, the complex and glittering patterns of romance can sometimes reduce the father-guide to a minor or less effective role. A tutor like Atlantes, who tries to shield his pupil from life, or a minor character like Guyon's Palmer, cannot be considered a major part of this tradition. On the other hand, the greatly increased importance of God the Father in ordinary life cannot easily be reflected in epic. The classical supernatural, still considered a necessary part of the genre, not only competes with Christianity, but has the advantage of being more immediately accessible just because the classical gods are so much more anthropomorphic.

However, there is a strand in the tradition which cuts across motifs, denies oppositions between natural and supernatural, male and female, and prepares us for a fuller use of the Christian God. Athena, Beatrice, Godfrey, and the Faerie Queene, as specific characters, seem to partake of both human and divine qualities, and impart a mysterious resonance to human existence that raises it above the limited categories by which it has been defined. An increased attentiveness to the muse, especially in Spenser, also adumbrates a new relationship with the divine. But the obvious Father-Son relationship available in Christianity, which, in the Incarnation, changed the terms of human life, has not yet been boldly used.

Heavenly messengers, the underworld, and prophecy all extend the hero's consciousness. Together with the use of fathers and sons, they also show us the care with which epic is built. One goes to the past in order to reaffirm it at its best, to contrast it with the less illustrious present, and to transform it into a contemporary vision. Within the epic, sons go to their fathers to learn, first, an awareness of the essential human condition, whatever may be there when all else is stripped away; that awareness may be simply of the value of the continuity of life. Father and son prove this reciprocally. Anchises has to be persuaded to leave Troy. The experience of Priam and Achilles is mutual. Hector and Aeneas care about the continuity of their people, but it is made more immediate for them in their sons.

The existence of generations is a basis for criticism. Primitive Florence claims a purity that criticizes the city of Dante. Heroes are never as strong and brave as once they were. The epic may be set in a past distanced from the time of the poet, so that it can become a criticism of his own time. The tradition that tries to conserve the past does so in order to make the present more aware of its deficiencies, its own departures from the possible. So past and present are a continuous pressure upon one another from which the future is born. The future, already pre-figured in the past, may be thought of by the poet with a good deal of dread. For the hero, it contains labor, exile, suffering, death; any hopes, for further adventures, dreams, or empires, are qualified by this knowledge. Fear is not conquered, but at the end the hero accepts a new beginning.

Perhaps there is always an element of divinity in the figure of the father. By turning to his father, the hero can transcend himself, but that aspect of divinity is also misleading. Anchises' prophecies can be incorrect. The classical gods themselves indicate the limitations of man's idea of the divine. The father is simultaneously to be venerated and suspected of excessive paternalism. The best "fathers" are those, like Athena and Beatrice, who leave the hero free to fulfill himself, and make themselves more an imaginative than a literal presence. They teach a freedom from historical categories that enables them to be more rather than less seriously involved in human con-

cerns. Fathers and sons, or guides and pilgrims, are dependent upon one another, on the one hand, for this
liberation from category, and, on the other, for the capacity
to commit the energy of liberation to creative activity in
the world.

6. *Identity*

> Thee I re-visit now with bolder wing,
> Escap't the *Stygian* Pool, though long detain'd
> In that obscure sojourn, while in my flight
> Through utter and through middle darkness borne
> With other notes then to th'*Orphean* Lyre
> I sung of *Chaos* and *Eternal Night*,
> Taught by the heav'nly Muse to venture down
> The dark descent, and up to reascend,
> Though hard and rare. . . .
>
> [3.13–21]

The epic as poem engages in the same experiences that
its characters do. That is, we can talk about the relationship between the author and his work in the same way that
we can discuss the hero and his task. The epic itself becomes experience while the poet-narrator becomes the hero.
Dante is explicitly the hero of his poem, achieving total
consciousness through study of the faults and virtues of
other men, and through the self-mirroring created by his
pairing with Vergil, his mentor and other self. But Dante
understood the validity of his use of himself partly by
studying the *Aeneid,* and seeing that Vergil had thought

of his poem as an epic task. Ariosto is the only possible hero of his poem, repeatedly calling attention to the great labor of the task of weaving the multiple strands of the *Orlando Furioso*. Without him there is no coherence: it is his heroic labor that holds the poem together.

The poem that shows man his mortality shows it first to the bard, and first affords immortality to the blind (mortal) bard through his gift. The epic poem also strikingly describes the mortal-immortal nature of man, and his self-consciousness, in the nature of its creation. Like no other genre, the epic cannibalizes itself, mirrors its predecessors, and passes judgment on them.[40] This innovation has to be ascribed to Vergil, who works with the *Iliad* and the *Odyssey* as though they were composed of movable parts, creating out of them his own poem. The method accomplishes a number of different things simultaneously. First, in its own way it demonstrates mortality. The *Iliad* and the *Odyssey* obviously do not die as man does, yet they do come out of a culture that is dead, and part of their continued interest is their place in their tradition, rather than simply in their own time. Like many Italian artists after him, Vergil saw ancient art as stuff to be torn down and recreated. He enabled Homer's poems, like people, to live on in their descendants. His acceptance of their impermanence made them permanent in their flexibility, in the way in which the *Aeneid* is only and uniquely itself, yet contains and reminds us of the past. It imitates death and resurrection.

Obviously the method demonstrates Vergil's self-consciousness, his understanding of the epic task, and his sense of kinship with Homer. It gives him ready-made common ground; in any way he chooses he can reflect

Homer's stories. The story of Dido is, for example, an ironic repetition of Nausikaa's, the idyllic pastoral transformed into a sophisticated seduction: the reader should anticipate that, if Odysseus left Nausikaa, it is likely that Aeneas will leave Dido. Vergil's poem is a transforming mirror of the earlier works. After Vergil, it is assumed that such mirroring will take place,[41] and the reader can find in the game of tracing analogies a way of regarding history itself as a set of prototypes existing transformed in the present, and shedding light upon it. The epic is thus a training ground for life, preaching conservative revolution: all must change, yet the past and the present are one.

The first six books of the *Aeneid* are Odyssean; the last six are Iliadic, and they are also made to match and reflect one another in an elaborate parallelism. Thus in this hall of mirrors, not only do the poems of Homer and Vergil face and illuminate one another; the two halves of Vergil's poem do the same thing, and while they reflect each other we see mirrored within them the Homeric stories. After Vergil every epic in this tradition revises and mirrors its predecessors.

When we stare at this chain of epics, then, what we should see first is the interrelationships among all these hero-poets and their poems—the ways in which all the poems reflect, attack, and fulfill one another. This is one genre in which T. S. Eliot's belief in the moving power of tradition is not only right but definitive; each additional epic changes its predecessors, consciously and explicitly. The *Aeneid* becomes more itself by taking on the *Iliad* and the *Odyssey;* yet having done so, in some sense it no longer needs them. It has been said that Milton ended the epic tradition: he did so no more than any other epic poet.

Like them, he translated his predecessors into his own world, where they are both necessary and superfluous.

Having begun by looking at the whole chain, we can then see that the story in the epic matches the story of the epic. What the legendary hero does is like what the poet does: he becomes self-conscious by putting himself into mirroring relationships with things and people. As we can look into the epic at the hero's story, he can look within it into his story mirrored on walls, in songs, in games— and no doubt within these games are further games, so that infinity is achieved by the repeated diminishing reflections, just as it is by the unending succession of the epic chain in time. This is a way of explaining why the epic hero's task is not the completion of a material goal. In fact, his work is to free the mind from such goals by showing that they do not count. What matters is the process of accepting mortality and then using mortality to transcend itself, using separation to achieve union.

As life is always in a state of becoming, so is the epic. Though, following Aristotle, critics have tried to describe it as a finished form with rules, even one of the first rules conceived of—*in medias res*—denotes its lack of any easily defined beginning, middle, and end. The length of the poem itself and the complexity of its historical-mythical context allow it to plunge into the midst of things with more apparent abandon than most other forms; loose ends can be referred to history or to other epics, or to some other book in the same epic. It would be fallacious to say that the *in medias res* opening intentionally imitates human life, yet the device, especially in the perspective of the chain of epics, inevitably gives the reader that impression. Human beings can get their bearings through the study of history. Epic contains the past in at least two different ways—in recovering the history of its own action, and in providing recollections of epics of the past. For the latter, the later the epic, the more history it can encompass, just as the later each man exists in time the longer the life he can achieve vicariously.

Nothing is ever completed neatly. The hero wants to achieve some goal, yet his own education—the situations in which he is involved in process—is what really matters. The poet's attitude toward his poem frequently is affected by dissatisfaction and a sense of incompleteness. Vergil on his deathbed is said to have asked that his poem be burned: its last lines have always struck readers as remarkably abrupt and harsh. Tasso wrote in pain and uncertainty, almost killing his poem by revising it according to the dictates of his critics. Spenser's *Faerie Queene* remains uncompleted; its total openness is epic.

There is also inevitably a sense of ongoingness in the epic, if only because of its length. The reader is aware of its being written over a long period of time, and often the original readers or hearers were sharing a work in progress: such was probably true of Homer's poems and certainly of Ariosto's and Spenser's. It may be difficult for the reader, then or now, to grasp the whole action. Calculated stoppings and startings, repetitious or interlaced episodes, and multiple jumps from one episode to another often seem positively to defy comprehension. We think it characteristic of art to provide for us a "stay against confusion,"[42] to eliminate the clutter of irrelevance that makes up so much of daily life. Despite appearances, the epic does achieve this purpose. Its complexity is not a jumbling of the details of real life, but a strenuous effort to render the frustration and the grandeur of heroic thought, which is always outstripping itself in impressive attempts to conceive and grasp new wholes.

The openness of epic beginnings is consistent with their conclusions. The author has tried to write a comprehensive work, for which in one lifetime there is rarely a second chance. Obviously the poem ends with a perspective wider than that with which it begins, but its conclusion may also be extremely inconclusive, ambiguous, or even lacking. It cannot be wholly coincidental that the writer's last work on epic is often done just before his death. Young men do not write epics before going on to other things, nor is an epic often put aside because it is finished to the author's satisfaction: it is in process as long as he is.

In medias res, then, is one way to describe the whole of an epic, not just its beginning. It is a narrative, a story, yet it begins in the middle and never concludes. The medium, and the means, are their own justification. The poem is like those ocular deceptions that Renaissance people were so fond of. It does have a beginning, a middle, and an end: battles are fought and won, marriages occur, heroes come home. Yet to give all one's attention to some glorious, palpable achievement is the preoccupation of minds tuned to chronology and climax. The epic allows this preoccupation to be satisfied; at the same time, it insists upon the inadequacy of such a viewpoint and encourages the reader to find other rewards.

The human condition, as portrayed in epic, suggests what seems to be a universal sense of a split between action and contemplation, aspects in eastern thought of yin and yang. The union of the two is the ideal; their separation and degradation are the norm. Epic attempts to identify the danger points, on the one hand, as concentration on specific worldly goals, and, on the other, as relapse into the debased garden state. In western tradition, the idea of achievement has always been the most compelling and dangerous: therefore, the epic simultaneously admires and undermines physical conquest, and stresses self-discovery. The ideal of contemplation, associated for us with the garden, is traditionally more congenial to eastern thought, and is seldom the direct goal of an epic character. Its dangers are sensuous self-abandon and idleness. The epic hero is almost always tempted to recoil against the mindless violence that is usually at least a part of his culture, by resorting to another kind of mindlessness, as discussed earlier —in the garden, suicide, or madness. But he survives. True self-knowledge, in these epics, is always arduously and consciously earned, not achieved by mystical or anti-intellectual modes of contemplation. Yet we have seen that there is a pattern of movement away from primitive formlessness, toward self-assertion, and then away from that into a more conscious form of integration with a whole. This narrative pattern is structurally supported.

Pulling against our narrative expectations—against the real existence of story in every epic—is a nonnarrative structure that implicitly explains problems raised by exclusive attention to chronological events. The *Iliad*'s many books devoted to battle details appear redundant if one is judging them as part of a sequence progressing toward a goal. However, if their purpose is to satiate the reader with the details of bloody warfare, then it becomes more difficult to judge how much is enough. The poem can be read as a series of passionate scenes, beginning with the strife between Achilles and Agamemnon. The battle sequences occupy the middle of the poem; their intention is to give us the feel of war and enable us as fully as possible to appreciate the concluding embrace of Achilles and Priam. It is as though those battle scenes were intended as a perspective glass through which to view a final symbolic portrayal of the best to which man can bring himself in this life.

Spenser designed his poem as a wheel, in which the action, instead of following in a simple line, rays out from its center and Gloriana's court, and then, in some way not arrived at by the poem, returns to that center again. The *Faerie Queene* is a game played upon a wheel-shaped board, with each knight advancing or retreating along its spokes according to the cast of the dice announced in successive stanzas. Arthur appears to travel in a circle around the rim. Although he is supposed to be in search of the Faerie Queene, from whose court each of the other knights has come, he neither asks nor receives directions. The circular movement itself is a way of getting there. Ariosto saw his poem as a web woven by the artist who finds the most compelling reason for life in the pleasure that he takes in his control over the story which so aggressively refuses a simple chronological line, but weaves in and out with the greatest, almost perverse, complexity imaginable.

The alternating viewpoint with which one is permitted to look at epic—the *trompe l'oeil* patterning—trains the mind and eye for the reintegration of the apparent opposites of action and contemplation. It works like a perspective picture of the interchanging patterns of figure and ground. We can neither stay with the story nor rest in the pattern; the story is not only an account of progress toward a goal, nor is the pattern a static rendering of experience. The story undercuts the value of action; the pattern is made up of unceasing motion. The ideal life of man, in which action and thought, body and soul, are integral with one another, is being restored, or achieved, by the demands that the poem makes upon the reader. As with immortality, by giving up the false contemplation represented by the Bower of Bliss, man learns true contemplation by immersing himself in the active pattern of life.

The poems also contain moments of transcendence which the characters themselves achieve in time. Dante's whole poem could be said to be such a moment, and any epic poet calling upon the muse is asking, on behalf of his art, for this power. In a lesser way, the dreams and visions frequent in epic are transcendent moments that teach the characters how to live in time, free of its power. Finally, there are infrequent moments of arbitrary, unexpected joy in the midst of life, such as occurs to Hector when he knows himself to be completely happy in battle. Such, also, is the vision of the Graces glimpsed by Calidore on Acidale. Colin Clout believes that the Graces bestow their gift arbitrarily; at any rate, there is no way in which it can be won by traditional heroic achievement.

By now it must be apparent that "traditional heroic achievement," while seen by none of these writers as unnecessary or invalid, always goes side by side with less obvious but at least equally important psychological achievement. Battles and empires may be won, but their celebration is not the dominant emotion with which we take leave of the poem. Just as the epic begins in the midst of things, so it never really comes to an end. Comedy formally concludes with marriages; the process of tragedy is symbolized by death. If there is any way of generalizing about epic, one may say that it is summed up in an embrace. Prototypical is the meeting in the *Iliad* between the enemies Priam and Achilles. The embrace is as moving and painful as anything in literature; its intention is mutual recognition of life's sorrow, of the oneness of all men in suffering. And it is not something that simply happens to fit at the end of the poem; like the deaths of tragedies, it has been made inevitable by and interprets for us the whole story of the poem. Priam is the controlled and insufficient old civilization; Achilles is uncontrolled primitive energy, newness, the destructive force that remaking requires. For help in their suffering, they have no one else to whom to turn than to each other, for each has the resources that the other needs. Their powers have destroyed each other, but they are used now for mutual affirmation, and for affirmation of the power and value of life. This is a step beyond anything that consciousness alone can achieve for itself, although it could not have been taken without the help of the kind of consciousness that is at work in the poem. It puts together all that the poet's consciousness had laid out in the poem, and finds that the whole is greater than the sum of its parts. It takes us not back to the inchoate beginnings of things from which the heroic consciousness emerges, but to a goal that is a new kind of wholeness and a new beginning.[43]

This is emphasized in a different way by the embrace of Penelope and Odysseus in Ithaca, which is simultaneously qualified and deepened by the slaughter that lies behind them and by our knowledge that Odysseus will continue to adventure, that he will not rest there in his hard-won home. All that Penelope and Odysseus ever did was made possible by their knowledge of each other, yet they are not the same selves they were before, and now they are like two worlds embracing. Odysseus' safety was dependent on her, not just at the last but throughout the poem, as she enabled the unconscious world to open itself to him. Their wholeness is portrayed traditionally as the union of male and female, which here carries with it all the archetypal associations of the words. Less impressive, though very similar, is the gift of Venus to the seafaring Portuguese when they find the island in the sea. Their maleness is complemented in the femaleness of the nymphs, and their restless consciousness in oceanic peace. From this union Venus hopes to create a new kind of people, combining strength with beauty, to inhabit the realms of Neptune from which she herself emerged. The mariners have to go back to Portugal, but it seems that they will take the nymphs with them. So the tension is not the parting of lovers, but the opposing pulls of their origins in land and sea. Like Venus, the poem hopes that a new kind of person will be born, but it cannot record the event.

Another characteristic epic marriage, which is a type of the embrace, is the betrothal of Redcrosse and Una, after only one portion of the unfinished *Faerie Queene*. Their betrothal is what their whole experience with each other in Fairyland has made possible, as they learn to complement each other, and strengthen rather than undermine each other's weaknesses. Like Odysseus, Redcrosse can now go on to many new adventures, for which he is better prepared than he was. But neither looks forward to a very secure future. The moment of wholeness in the epic is brief and fragile. Just when the war is over and problems seem solved, the wedding of Ruggiero and Brada-

mante is interrupted by the challenge and killing of Rodomonte. Rodomonte dies cursing and goes to Hell, and
further wars and fighting are inevitable. We are never
allowed to think, "happily ever after."

The "embrace" between Turnus and Aeneas is a death-
grip, signifying among other things the obliteration of the
Trojan race. Yet placed as it is at the very end of the
poem, with no mitigating concluding words at all, it emphasizes a perspective that we cannot very well do without. Aeneas has all along portrayed the civilizing force
of the new Rome coming into existence; that is what he
has been educated into in the first six books. Yet, just as
there he inherited the dominant characteristics of those
who had to be sacrificed, here in the last books of the
poem he has been exhibiting many signs of Turnus' primitive energy. Turnus has often in the poem been compared
to Achilles, and Aeneas has been called *pater* since the
death of Anchises. Thus they re-enact, with heavy irony,
the scene between Achilles and Priam. At least that was a
moment of affirmation, after warfare and suffering. This
approaches rejection of any human encounter. Troy must
lose its name and language; Turnus must lose his life.
The old Troy and the primitive Italy will merge into a
new anonymous whole. Humanity is foregone for the sake
of humanity. The piety remains (Aeneas kills Turnus out
of piety); the primitive energy remains (his own energy
is directed against Turnus); and we are forced to acknowledge the great human importance of Turnus to the whole
poem. But both piety and energy are so victimized by the
idea of empire that one is forced to at least qualify severely
the value one can assign to that idea.

Dante picked Vergil for his poet partly because he admired the concept of a world united by empire, but he makes Vergil call his own poem a tragedy, and himself abandons all worldly enterprise. Like Odysseus and Penelope, he and Beatrice pull into the male-female archetypes all the associated opposites with which they belong, and, much more explicitly than with Penelope, the power of Beatrice enables Dante's journey.

We have seen that the concept of a place of final wholeness exists as the opposite of the original cave. As the cave has come to represent not just original formlessness but a repository of all the unconscious and repressed fears and passions of the human mind, the imagined Heaven is a place of bliss, won by the use of consciousness to transcend itself. That state of fulfillment, however, is all but unimaginable, and its description is beyond the resources of language. The hero, recognizing that he cannot go back and still retain his humanity, nevertheless mistakenly seeks respite in false paradises and willed oblivion. Only rarely in epic does the true Paradise appear, as vision of the future in the *Faerie Queene*, and as Dante's briefly visited Paradiso.

Thus the epic embrace is of such major and definitive importance. Painful, partial, or momentary as it may be, it is also seen as worth everything. For this, although he may not entirely realize it, the hero became human and played his part in life. Obviously, it is a symbol of the reconciliation of opposites, and of self-transcendence. Jung gives this symbolic interpretation of marriage,[44] and Christian mysticism has always used the figure in an equivalent way, as a portrayal of the marriage of Christ with the soul. That experience is at the absolute limit of epic possibility. For, although it is true that the tradition does involve the supernatural, it never does so in a way that excludes possible human experience. If Aeneas is half-divine and Dante is united with a heavenly Beatrice, that is a way of saying that humanity can transcend itself in its own flesh. The power of the epic is its recounting of the strength that humanity has to raise itself from unconsciousness, accept the terms of mortality, and then discover that the full acceptance of those conditions enables transcendence of them. That is when spirit shines through flesh. The limitations of humanity are never more obvious than when Odysseus and Penelope embrace in a house of death. Because of these limitations, the story of their achievement endures.

There are heroes in the poem, and the poem is heroic, written by a poet-hero who embraces his counterparts in the tradition. The hero learns to know himself in spiritual journeying, in mirroring encounters with others. He learns what he has to do to fulfill himself in a world that is limited and places limits on him. He accepts his historical destiny, knowing what it is. And the epic poet accepts it for him, knowing and demonstrating its often tragic dimensions. The hero pushes the boundaries of consciousness out beyond that: the selfhood that he pioneers in time, and the transcendence of selfhood, are what matter. The poem is both active and contemplative, having a narrative and a nonnarrative pattern. It celebrates destruction and creation both in the actions of its characters and in its own participation in epic tradition. The paradoxical inextricability of these forces is complemented by many other such unions, in an existence that cannot be godlike without being mortal, creative without destruction and death, intellectual without love, male without female, active without contemplation, communal without separation. Epic makes every demand upon the solitary mind, asking it first to define itself and learn to preserve its own integrity, and then, in seeking to reach beyond reason, to blur its boundaries again. As we read, the boundaries of the poems themselves blur, episodes are transformed into different episodes, characters from one poem find their descendants in another, and the interpretations of whole poems take on new depths in the changing flow and play of consciousness from age to age. This series of mirrors within mirrors is the tradition inherited by Milton.

II

Paradise Lost

I have been looking at the epic in terms of a number of suppositions that deeply occupy the human mind. Every epic is built on some basic assumptions about the nature of reality—that consciousness emerges out of an encompassing source which in varying degrees inhibits, threatens, or nourishes it; that a person cannot be recognizably human unless he differentiates himself from that source, but separation brings about alienated opposites where there once was wholeness; and that for human beings consciousness involves awareness of death. Epic characters and epic poets have tasks to accomplish within the context of a given society, but the poem is more subversive of its society than has been ordinarily believed: the hero's task is performed and his society is accepted because there is no other, but it is always clear that neither the culture nor its preservation is as important as self-conflict and self-knowledge. The real task is to accept his own mortality, and then to transcend it, avoiding those illusive havens which seem to offer shelter from a hopeless world. The hero's education through art, through human relationships, and through contemplation teaches him to surpass awareness by means of awareness. Assuming consciousness to be a given and life worthwhile, epic suggests patterns of reconciliation enabling opposites to recover wholeness in one another and life to be affirmed even by means of death, in a momentary transcendence.

Probably a condition of the greatest epic poetry is that its author lives in a particularly spacious age, when both past and future are already more available than usual. No epic poet previous to Milton lived at a more crucial turning point in history. Crisis was both created and exacerbated by the sudden jump in human individuation that took place during the sixteenth and seventeenth centuries. To some people of the time, and to many in subsequent centuries, the Renaissance seemed to be an exodus from the cave of the Middle Ages, a time when the arts and sciences could flourish as they had not done since ancient times. Every man could read the Bible for himself and try to work out his own salvation. Yet to Milton, living impatiently in the latter part of this great age, it seemed as though time had run out without being rightly used.

He was as self-conscious as any epic poet had ever been, and, before 1660, convinced as none of them had ever been before that God at this time intended, through human agents, to make things new. The rhetoric of his antiprelatical tracts, written in the 1640s, contains image clusters that graphically present his view of human existence at that time. All "external things" are repressive and evil: Milton constantly attacks disproportion and opposition between inner and outer meaning. Sometimes the appearance of grace conceals its opposite, as is the case with cosmetics, church vestments, rituals both of action and of language. Sometimes imagery of external disorder emphasizes the inner condition: here he uses metaphors of deformity, disease (especially skin disease), and nausea.[1]

In either case, the outer shell, like a cave, covers a dark interior.

Tasso thought that a poem could only be as good as the world of which it was a part,[2] and perhaps, in his earlier days, Milton agreed. In the 1640s he said that his great poem would not usher in the new society; rather, it would await that society's birth and the creation of readers capable of understanding it (3.1, 148). Thus, unlike previous epic poets, Milton was not going to undermine his own celebration. Instead, he would help to realize a society worthy of epic praise. Some forecast of the song that would then be possible is given us in the "Nativity Ode," in which Milton, at twenty-one, celebrates God's renewal of the world. And there are frequent glimpses, in the polemical prose, of that idyllic future date. Milton never expected to spend twenty years of his life writing propaganda for a failing cause, and, when he finally became free to write his epic, it had to be built on the experience of heroic failure.

During those twenty years, Milton saw himself as a participant in, and a recorder of, epic in the making. He acted out in reality some of the familiar assumptions of traditional epic—that evil can be overcome, great new societies constructed, and men and women enabled to be free and happy when released from external bondage. His most interesting depiction of the process is the *Second Defense of the English People*, a work which he defines as oration and compares to epic. It is formally oration—a defense, to the world, of England's regicide; he compares the oration to epic because it praises one great action of revolutionary heroism. As one ponders the significance of the execution, to Milton and his allies, it becomes more and more apparent that it had to happen, but not because it was right or legal, for it was not, despite all Milton's claims. For the regicides it was an event as symbolic as the fall of Troy, a portrayal of the end of the medieval order, a destruction of the image of paternal and transcendent authority for the sake of a new age. This one action insured that not even the Restoration could enable a real return to the old order. By an act of illegality and violence, the country irrevocably committed itself to the primacy of law and individual conscience. Yet Milton, in the 1660s, could not have known that this would be so. For him there was only that short period of great hope followed by disillusionment.

Vergil depicts his hero turning in blind defeat from the burning city, unwilling to face the future and incapable of understanding what he has to do. Milton himself put the torch to his city, and in his prose tracts recreated his world. He redesigned the church, the university, marriage, and the state, building from within. He rejected tradition, rejected all that he called "external things," and, rejecting them, gave up the framework of society that had enabled other epic poets to test their own beliefs. Milton could test nothing; all must be made new, and therefore the new models would be put into operation as the revolution began to succeed. First this, then the poem.

He wrote the *Second Defense* as though the new world were so nearly realized that oration was epic in the making, and Milton the pamphleteer an epic hero. He gives thanks for having been born at a time in history when his country's citizens, after "setting examples and performing deeds of valour, the greatest since the foundation of the world, delivered the Commonwealth from a grievous domination, and religion from a most debasing thraldom" (8.3), and for having been chosen to defend his cause against its formidable European opponent, the Royalist scholar Salmasius. For these two, as for many of their contemporaries, the written word was an extension of the self, subject to the same treatment, including execution by burning at the stake, and banishment. Wars were fought in language as well as on the battlefield, and Milton sees himself dueling, first with Salmasius and then with More, for the honor of his cause, for the commonwealth against the old order.

The personal abuse that these two strangers hurl at each other is characteristic of the time,[3] and, for Milton, even stitches together his personal and his public life. Defending his countrymen, he defends himself, styling himself John Milton, Englishman, a fit title for an epic hero. More extensively here than anywhere else, he gives the details of his life in its coherent commitment to liberty. He had earlier covenanted with the people and with God that when the society was renewed he would be its poet, and he had said that the poet must himself be a great poem. Both as bard and as Englishman, he makes himself a figure of the commonwealth.

The second section of the *Defense* is devoted to encomia of major actors in the revolution—Bradshaw (the judge at the trial of Charles), Fairfax, Cromwell, and others. They are the architects of law and liberty, the exemplars of self-fulfillment. But already Milton is thinking beyond military accomplishment to what he calls the harder victories of peace. Just as all the epics of the past undermined their own cultures even while they praised them, Milton warns that further wide-sweeping reforms are essential to the maintenance of liberty. Thus, while the tract is set forth as a defense of the English against their foreign detractors, it is also a warning to the English of their own deficiencies. They had not yet achieved separation of church and state, freedom from censorship, abolition of old restrictive legislation, and sufficient popular education. But they had already gone as far as they would ever go in Milton's lifetime. In the early years of the Restoration, Milton found himself a blind, jobless, fifty-two-year-old ex-convict, a widower with three young daughters. Now, facing a hostile world, he was very much in the position of Aeneas leaving Troy, Dante exiled from Florence, except that he was older and, in his blindness, more destitute than they. He had lived one epic, and was writing another.

In earlier years, Milton had thought his subject would be King Arthur. That once and future king was of all English monarchs the most unkillable, and must have seemed to the disillusioned regicide the antithesis of the kind of hero who was called for now. However, the greatest problem with which Milton had to wrestle was not the existence of royal tyranny, but the ingratitude of a people who would reject the freedom offered them at such cost. William Riley Parker speculates that when Milton began *Paradise Lost,* "during the closing years of the Commonwealth, he probably envisaged the epic as a parable on mankind's gift, through divine grace, of a *second chance,* and on the need for learning how to put first things first." [4] Only when deprived of his patriotic vision of the commonwealth as second chance could he have written an epic in the great tradition, still imbued with revolutionary consciousness, but now drawn on a cosmic plan.

Milton's poetry demands to be set both in its literary context and in this historical context of his own life. *Paradise Lost* and *Paradise Regained* continue the attack on external things which for him had been the cause of revolution. His opponents had been, first, tradition, and then men's love of their own bondage. In the poetry he continues this warfare, and adds one new kind of opponent to which we would give the name "technocracy." Like many of his contemporaries, Milton deeply distrusted that aspect of science which distracts men from themselves. It is a way to avoid putting first things first.

An awareness both of epic tradition and of Milton's historical perspectives can significantly affect one's first encounter with Satan. In the lines said to have almost caused denial of publication,[5] Satan overlooking his cohorts is compared to a doomed king:

> As when the Sun new ris'n
> Looks through the Horizontal misty Air
> Shorn of his Beams, or from behind the Moon
> In dim Eclips disastrous twilight sheds
> On half the Nations, and with fear of change
> Perplexes Monarchs.
>
> [1.594–99]

The lines not only foreshadow Satan's own defeat, but challenge that divine-right tradition whose stock metaphor was the comparison of God, King, and Sun, equating that tradition with resistance to change. Absolute rejection of Satan's own status as magnificent rebel is intended, although that rejection may at first come hard.

For the poem opens in a cave. With no opportunity even to awaken in a dark wood, much less to grasp the context of the world which this cave may serve or threaten, the reader is simply thrown into it, along with Satan. And this is not the original womb of consciousness, but the much more sinister cave of the present moment, created by Satan, King Charles, and the English people. It is Ariosto's world and Dante's Inferno. Milton begins in the cave and locates the reader within its confines because it is the human condition, and might as well be reckoned with at once. Although at the outset it is physically limited and inhabited only by Satan's forces, Milton makes apparent in many ways throughout the poem that Hell now rules earth. As in Dante, humans are doubly encaved— because that is where they live, and because they do not know it.

The poet makes a bold and trustful choice in opening this way, giving us extensive first impressions of both God and Satan from Satan's point of view. Milton always assigns his villains the most exciting oratory, but with Satan he outdoes himself, and, even with the poet's own corrective voice, whole generations of readers have believed that God is a tyrant, who rules by custom. Always before, the stuff of the cave has been seen from outside, as a threat; now we ourselves become the "threat," are allowed to identify our consciousness with Satan's, and everything appears in reverse. The poem opens in the cave to remind its readers that they are fallen and cannot trust themselves; nor can they trust Satan; nor can they trust the poet, unless he is inspired by the divine muse, of which there is no guarantee. On the eve of the Restoration, Milton, in his pamphlets, tried to dissuade his countrymen from submitting to an alien authority. Now, himself subject to that authority, he is still urging people to see where they are, and to take responsibility for themselves.

One can easily see the ways in which the poem establishes a continuity with the *Faerie Queene* and its Blatant Beast. In Milton's poem, as in Spenser's, language both seduces and saves. Satan's angels land in Hell because they are persuaded by the words of Satan set against the creating Word of God. And this descent carries us far beyond the maraudings of the Blatant Beast; although language remains an essential part of this Hell, the death of language can be seen here too. It is a place of repressed, distorted knowledge, chosen oblivion, static and meaningless violence. Everyone has noticed the nihilistic character of its description—flames without light, bottomless perdition, and torture without end are its materials: it is simultaneously the last great rendition of an external devils' Hell and a psychological portrayal of a tormented mind. If God is everything, then Satan in his perversity must choose to come as close to being nothing as he can.

Neither he nor his troops will admit what they have done. Their anxiety to believe that Hell is a quite acceptable piece of real estate is only another illustration of what they have been doing to their minds ever since Satan conceived of Sin. Even when Beelzebub intends to recall them to reality from their delusions, he does it by asking them sarcastically whether they wish to be styled princes of Hell, which of course they already are. Milton tells us that they have lost the capacity for reality (6.115), and they cannot be saved because, like the sinners in Dante's *Inferno,* they choose at every moment to be what and

where they are. The repeated eating of the fruit of ash in
Book 10 is a final illustration of that.

The real fount of original unconsciousness has little to
do with this sophisticated, willed alienation. It is what
Milton calls Chaos, and to discuss it requires also discussion of Milton's God, whose identity is creator, and whose
building material this is. It would in fact be meaningless
to Milton to ask what God was doing before creation;
making things is his reason for being and the only means
by which he can be recognized. But the act of creating
something not oneself is a way of bringing about self-
consciousness, and Milton portrays God as enduring this
experience, subject to the same limitations or requirements
that beset other conscious beings.

Milton's God is the mystery at the heart of the universe, and of this poem, impossible to describe in human
language.[6] Yet Milton keeps describing him as best he
can, and the majority of our problems with the poem stem
from the inadequacy of words in this respect. God is not a
person or a character, but a direction and a force for life.
In the poem we apprehend only aspects of him, like the
Son, the God of Book 3, and the figures of light which at
the opening of Book 3 imitate the mystery of many-faceted
Deity. Yet if we are constantly mistaking the part for the
whole, that is not just because the whole is incompre-
hensible. It is also because God as creator is committed to
these partial manifestations of himself in history.

That for Milton the mainspring of life is creative is un-
deniable. For us, creativity implies consciousness, and
being like our own. One cannot speak of "God" without
using pronouns. In order to talk about *Paradise Lost*, one
has to accept these difficulties and then try to transcend

them. Milton's God is a creative consciousness, a force that is comprehensive but not all-knowing or omnipotent in any human sense. In its own endurance of consciousness, it experiences states analogous to human ones, and so can be roughly and inaccurately described in human terms. In going back to the origins of things, Milton tried to antici-pate human consciousness. The archetypal myth, the story of creation, is the story of God's discovery of himself, and therefore of otherness and death. If God were a person, he would be the primary hero of the poem.[7] As it is, we see in him the stuff from which our concept of heroism is derived.

He does not, like the orthodox Christian God, create from nothing, and so he is peculiarly handicapped, and made more interesting at the same time. God's conscious-ness at the beginning emerged from or coexisted with Chaos,[8] the Abyss, which is described as the original cave, pit, vacuity, emptiness, "the Womb of nature and per-haps her Grave" (2.911). On this, the Spirit at creation brooded, and caused it to be pregnant (1.21–22). God could not make a perfect universe. He is given warring elements, and, when he creates, he has to purge out of them "the black tartareous cold Infernal dregs / Adverse to life" (7.237–38). Creation is not only separation of not-God from God; it is also separation of Chaos from form, dark from light. Creation causes oppositions and the potentiality of evil. Dividing the light from darkness, God "saw the light was good," but made no observation about the dark. Chaos is resistant to creation, at least as friendly to Satan as to God.

God makes nothing without the instrumentality of the Son; if created by God, he was created first, before all other things. The begetting of the Son is a manifestation, not a birth.[9] It is a reaffirmation of the Son's participation in the creation of other things and in their reconciliation to God. God cannot exist without making things; he cannot make without dividing; he cannot divide without longing for wholeness. Repeatedly, the begetting of the Son is explained in terms of unity:

> Under his great Vice-gerent Reign abide
> United as one individual Soule
> For ever happie. . . .

> [5.609–11]

The begetting of the Son and the birth of Sin happen almost at once, though neither in human time. Sin is a reaction to the Son on the part of Satan, who will not believe that he was created, will not believe himself to be part of an ongoing process, does not wish to think that he is different from God (which is what it means to have been created), or that he will again one day be a part of God through the reuniting power of the Son. So he turns violently away from the process of life: copulating with Sin, he creates Death; Death and Sin copulate in turn, creating more death. The rigidity of these allegorical figures brilliantly emphasizes the sterile rigidity of the kind of mind that has to conceive them.

In a way it is appropriate to say that Satan himself created Hell. Unable to bear the appearance of the Son, he and his angels flung themselves out of heaven, and fell to the place that their own minds contained. Yet it is also and simultaneously true that God's reaction to Satan's behavior is the creation of Hell. At this point God acknowledges that creativeness has produced (and must produce) evil, destructiveness, and death. The price of consciousness, of creativity, is knowledge of and participation in death, and, in some sense at least, God, like man, would prefer to reject that knowledge. Satan is sent as far away as possible and erased from the book of life. Yet Sin and Death, untrustworthy wardens, are given the guardianship of Hell. Once conscious of oppositions, one cannot deny their existence. And God, who is life, the maker of the oppositions, does not exist without them, at least not in relation to life that is not God.

As Milton tells us at the beginning, his poem is meant to justify the ways of God to men. The best way to define "justification," in the sense in which he means it, is as explanation. He would not try to defend God—that would be presumptuous; rather, his poem is meant to try to show more clearly who God is and why he has to work the way he does. So far, as we have seen, that means that *Paradise Lost* provides a theology of the cave. Where all other epic poems have caves that must be explored, they never say why the cave is necessary, difficult of access, and likely to be full of violence. Milton's whole poem explores this problem. One basic assumption is that God brought life out of Chaos, and that the process of creation therefore requires the realization of opposites, including death, the opposite of life itself. God himself, with regard to human beings, finds this knowledge scarcely bearable; it is no wonder that the human mind tries to conceal it from itself.

In all previous epic poems except Dante's and, in a sense, Ariosto's, the caves are enclosures, often subterranean, in the real world, of which they form a relatively minor though important part. Even Dante's Inferno is put in its place by the astronomical shift in viewpoint that Dante undergoes when he reaches the empyrean. But in Milton's poem, Heaven, earth, and Hell are themselves fragile enclosures, surrounded by, or jutting out into, Chaos. Of course Milton's poem is supposed to take place at the beginning of things, when formlessness perhaps occupied more territory than form. Still it is an unusual way of describing God's world. And there is every reason to believe Milton thought life in modern times to be at least as perilously balanced as, in his cosmology, it is at the beginning.

Like everything else in *Paradise Lost,* Milton's caves include all those of the tradition, because they come first in the mythology, although the poem was written last. The poem dealing with the first myth takes theological responsibility to explain why the world of the other epics must be as it is. God brought life out of Chaos, which never in itself is made to seem as desirable as, for example, Calypso's cave. God himself not only coexisted with, or perhaps even came from, Chaos; the production of anything touches off the creation of an opposite in the dialectic of life, and this will eventually lead to the naming of the fortunate fall: evil begins to seem lucky because it leads to good. But the first striking juxtapositions are those of Heaven, Hell, and Chaos. As soon as consciousness, in the form of God, or Heaven, comes up like a point of light out of Chaos, it also produces a dangerous depth below Chaos, which is Hell.

Creation liberates the mind from one kind of nothingness, only, it would seem, that it may fall prey to another of its own devising, the whole process then becoming further complicated by the innate ambiguities and obscurities of fallen life. Such demonstrations lead naturally enough to a setting forth of the ambiguities and errors of cultures, in a context worthy of the epic tradition that subtly undermines its own subject and heritage. Perhaps himself leaning on the precedent of Tasso's *Discourses*, Milton shamelessly pretends that war had been the literal subject of previous epics so that he can subvert it by making Satan into a mock ruler. In Books 1 and 2, he gives every possible advantage to Satan's tyrannic imagination, to the lure of all the marvellous trappings of the martyr-king, who has the dual psychological advantage of being both leader and underdog. The army fought Charles in the king's own name, on the assumption that he had been misled by his friends. It was hard for men as for angels to turn their backs on the Son of the Morning. Satan also has the stature and qualities of the oppressed and daring epic hero, of all epic heroes sorrowing for the plight of their followers, but determined not to yield.

It is less commonly noticed that the articulate, irritating God of Book 3 is also designed according to a classical model.[10] He is Homer's Zeus:

'Oh for shame, how the mortals put the blame upon us
gods, for they say evils come from us, but it is they, rather,
who by their own recklessness win sorrow beyond what is given.
. . . Aigisthos married
the wife of Atreus' son, and murdered him on his homecoming,
though he knew it was sheer destruction, for we ourselves had
   told him,
sending Hermes, the mighty watcher. . . .'

[*Odyssey*, 1.32–38]

Athena pleads for mercy for Odysseus, Zeus claims he has that particularly in mind, and Hermes is dispatched again to help. That aspect of Milton's God which has always seemed most disagreeable to hostile critics, his eagerness to exonerate himself of blame for an event which he knew would happen, is imitated and caricatured from Homer.

In discussing the epic poet's relationship with his culture, I have earlier described some ways in which he both celebrates and undermines his culture's ideals. Milton rejected out of hand the autocratic ideal of civic order as described by apologists as disparate as Hooker and Hobbes. And he not only rejected the established church before anything else; the opening lines of *Paradise Lost* tell us that the Spirit prefers "before all Temples th'upright heart and pure." He never found any church that was as well-designed. In Book 12 of the poem, Michael spells out the historical risks that must be taken by people who would do the will of God:

>   O that men
> (Canst thou believe?) should be so stupid grown,
> While yet the Patriark liv'd, who scap'd the Flood,
> As to forsake the living God, and fall
> To worship thir own work in Wood and Stone
> For Gods! yet him God the most High voutsafes
> To call by Vision from his Fathers house,
> His kindred and false Gods, into a Land
> Which he will shew him, and from him will raise
> A mightie Nation, and upon him showre
> His benediction so, that in his Seed
> All Nations shall be blest; he straight obeys,

Not knowing to what Land; yet firm believes:
I see him, but thou canst not, with what Faith
He leaves his Gods, his Friends, and native Soile. . . .

[12.115–29]

At a time when the destruction of all humanity is still a
living memory, when little indeed can have been achieved
in the way of ritual to give people a sense of historical
permanence, Abraham is asked to leave family, friends,
gods, and country, and set out he knows not where.
Milton's God demands of people this capacity to reject
tradition, external things, guides acquired even in the
immediate past. In turn, Milton's insistence on freedom
from man-made limitations demands the disciplined obedience to God which makes that freedom possible.

The God of Book 3 is an aspect of Milton's God, one
which many seventeenth-century people would have found
an acceptable portrayal of Deity. In context, he performs
several important functions. For one thing, he does provide that acceptable portrayal, under cover of which
Milton can work for its subversion. For another, he is a
companion-piece to Satan in a dual reflection on the limitedness of classical ideals. Satan is a criticism of the classical
hero; God criticizes classical gods. Immortality is all
very well, but it has a tendency to induce vanity and
superficiality, as readers of Homer always discover. Conceived of as immortal persons, fathers, or kings, gods
attract disrespect. Milton had nothing against kings in
general, but quite a lot against most kinds of kings. The
idea of perpetual reign, of static monarchy, was certainly
antipathetic to him. For those who may be satisfied with

such an idea, Milton allows the trappings to remain, just as Vergil allows empire to seem desirable, even though he wants his fit audience to see more clearly. It is at the point of this recognition that Milton's epic differs from others. Other epic poets undercut their given myths without suggesting any alternative vision. Dante comes closest with the spiritual community of the faithful that for him replaces community on earth. Like Dante, Milton is without immediate political hope, but he is less able than Dante to work with a given religious orthodoxy.

The most important function performed by the God of Book 3 is begetting (or exalting) the Son, and assigning to him the royal sceptre. This is a God who understands his own limitedness and is able to transcend it enough to submit himself to the larger power of God as life. Now, if held in mind, the parallel between Satan and Charles I as eclipsed sun-kings enables a true Miltonic perspective on both the English Revolution and the war in heaven. In announcing the begetting of the Son, God reveals himself as a creative, active, living force, while Satan, unwilling to risk his own status, attempts to freeze the hierarchy by replacing God. When the Son offers to become incarnate, and God gives throne and sceptre to the God-man, the direction of life becomes even more evident. It is that unifying, humanizing force to which Satan is opposed. The English revolutionists, fighting their war in the king's name, wanted to believe that their king could change with them, but that divine-right monarch could only be threatened by any change he could not control. Politically, it is the equation of Charles and Satan that is important and no other; from a Miltonic perspective, they are the impeders of life. From this perspective, the behavior of the

English people, rejecting popular government for the security of a monarch, or the behavior of Satan, rejecting the unifying power of the Son, does seem ungrateful. In this light, it is much easier to understand the hostile attitude of the God of Book 3.

It is also easier to understand both the execution of Charles and the freeing of Satan. Imprisoned, Charles I was meant as an idea to be relegated to oblivion, but that tactic could not work. He was actively trying to restore divine-right monarchy, and the execution was an effort to obliterate what Milton could only have seen as the power of death. By the time he began to write *Paradise Lost*, he recognized that, even after physical execution, Charles as an idea was an ineradicable power. Satan could not be executed, had to be left at large to his own dark designs. History, necessary to creation, could not be short-circuited. If God wanted to create, he had to subject himself to human limitations. Milton connects the political system under which he was born, and which he tried to overthrow, with that which Satan wants to inaugurate, or maintain. But he also criticizes the commonwealth's most central action by declaring it pointless to try to destroy evil. God lets Satan go, and the results are shown both in the catalog of devils in Book 1 and in Michael's recital of biblical history in Books 11 and 12.

History was not intended to happen at all. But since it did happen, it is given a much more prominent place, as history, in the poem than is usual for epic, occupying most of the last two books, instead of the less conspicuous earlier section that was often part of the hero's visit to the underworld. Having concluded that one cannot put one's faith in any political system, Milton now undercuts not one system but all. For all are, in the biblical sense, principalities, ruled by external things. Nevertheless, Books 11 and 12 are not pessimistic, for, unlike most epic writers, Milton does have an alternate plan of life to suggest. The facts of history as portrayed by Michael enable Adam and Eve to see it as made up of external things, and so to give it the kind of attention it deserves. Like their Christian descendants, they now have a record that allows them transcendence over history, in showing them its whole sweep, and an event (the Incarnation) that releases them from history in each moment. While time still has to be taken seriously because it is their only context for daily life, the place where they must work out their salvation, it is in a larger sense relieved of its importance. Nothing has to be done except the will of God, a task that does not depend on worldly contingencies. Worldly power loses its authority, and individual heroism, redefined by Milton as patience and heroic fortitude, becomes possible.

God and Satan, in very different ways, are both responsible for evil, but for God it is a by-product and a building-block, whereas it is Satan's whole intent. Human beings are asked to choose between creation and destruction, and the choice is never altogether clear. Things resemble their opposites. In his account of history, Michael provides an over-all pattern—life before the law, life under the law, and life in grace. Within this pattern what we notice is that individual access to life or death is both available and confused at any time. The flood that drowns humanity brings promise and renewal to the one just man. God works through Noah to recreate. Nimrod, on the other hand, taps the source of death, taking the bituminous material of Hell for bricks to build his tower. Those acts imitate original creation and original destruction. They look like the opposite of what they are. And they are real history, an atemporal working in time—that is to say, Milton rejects the false claims of chronological time in favor of *kairos,* epiphanic time,[11] and the readiness of each person for the right moment when it occurs.

The whole design of the poem is intended to imitate the release of the central forces of destruction and creation outward into their material realization in history as described at the beginning (in the catalog of devils) and at the end. It is usual in epic for history to be inspired by both the demonic and the divine, but Milton's perspective is new. The event in the garden is a human action, and it is the central event in the poem. The recounting of human history is given much more space than ever before. But it is clear that history, though necessary, is merely the outside manifestation of these cosmic forces. That is why the war in Heaven and the creation occupy the central books, exerting their pressure outward on the histories that begin and end the poem. The emphasis is on spiritual energy, the creative power of life, and the destructiveness of death, and human action is perverse unless it is concerned with these rather than with efforts either to settle down in comfort or to reach goals.

During Michael's account of history, the words "violent" and "violence" are used repeatedly;[12] in fact, the first act shown to Adam is the murder of Abel. And in the first part of this study, we saw that the hero is always vulnerable to the cave of his own passions which he must keep severely under control, especially at the end of the story. Often in earlier epic, executive and active force is divided between two characters—as Agamemnon and

Achilles, or Godfrey and Tancred. The executive character then assumes a godlike role, free of implication in
violence because he has someone else to do the acting for
him. Milton's God does not escape that easily. One may
say that Satan is God's rejected violence, and the Son is
his creative power. Satan's mind is a cave that Satan himself cannot escape, and he is the symbol of human bondage
to inner darkness. In the process of Incarnation, Christ
frees people from the necessity of that bondage, emphasizing physically the presence of God within, reidentifying
self-knowledge with God-knowledge. But God often
manifests contrary passions in his own being. There is a
cave near God's throne from which come both darkness
and light, so that there can be day and night in heaven.
Gunpowder can be discovered in heaven's underground.
God himself is a coincidence of opposites,[13] and his work
as creator shows it. Raphael tells Adam that when humanity was created, Raphael was guarding the gates of Hell
so that no spy or enemy should come forth while God
was working:

> Least hee incent at such eruption bold,
> Destruction with Creation might have mixt.
>
> [8.235–36]

When God sent the flood, Milton tells us in his *Christian
Doctrine*, he really did repent of having made man. The
whole poem of *Paradise Lost* is full of the word "lest"
and other equivalent constructions intended to express uncertainty. Although the poem implies continuous right
choices on God's part, it also offers continuous possibilities
for less attractive alternatives. Like his creatures, God has

to contend with the fact of the cave; if he wants to work in time, he too must be subject to time.

The cave does not equal Satan, even though the two go together in so many ways. The cave near God's throne is not the cave of Hell. It is true that earlier epics' galaxy of uncontrolled characters—pagans, Amazons, wild men, and so forth—are all adumbrated by Satan and his forces at the beginning of the poem, and in the many references throughout the poem to subsequent myth and history. Satan was once brother to all the angels, and himself a son of God, a fact that he tries to use in *Paradise Regained*. The dark energy that keeps getting assimilated into civilized order, to keep it going, is apparent in God, in whom darkness and light meet, and from whom Satan came. It is a characteristic of Eve, properly in balance with reason, but dangerous, like the creative spirit itself, when unmonitored. It is the stuff of "unpremeditated verse," woven into the most ordered, thoughtful iambic pentameter. Darkness, or whatever that mystery may be called, can be strongly bent to good or evil.

How, then, distinguish between God and Satan, between authentic and inauthentic inspiration? As Milton himself knew, that is extremely difficult, perhaps impossible for unaided human vision. But, in the poem, one way is to see that God includes and Satan excludes almost everything. Another is to look for process and movement. When the mind is given over to Hell, it cannot move even to escape despair and death. The fact that the narrator of the poem does not despair could in itself be proof of the validity of his gift.[14] God continues to create, affirming the goodness of life; the destruction he risks is incidental to his purpose.

Satan's purpose is negation. He chooses not-life, will not even name God. And while God might like not to know about Satan, he admits him to his knowledge and uses him as material with which to build his kingdom.

God never engages in unnecessary violence. That is nowhere more apparent than in his choice of the Son to end the war. The Son takes on God's hatred for his enemy in a deliberate way, and he scarcely has to do more than show himself in order for Satan and his troops to cast themselves into Hell. As soon as he appears, because he is the creative principle, destruction begins to be healed:

> At his command the uprooted Hills retir'd
> Each to his place, they heard his voice and went
> Obsequious, Heav'n his wonted face renewd,
> And with fresh Flourets Hill and Valley smil'd. . . .
>   [6.781–84]

Only then does he turn his attention to his enemies, and he does not really engage in warfare against them. His apocalyptic chariot, together with thunder and lightning, convinces them that they would be better off elsewhere.

So the pattern of a self-control that often spills over at the end is missing in this poem, partly because in Milton's epics there is no building up to a worldly goal. The heroism is shared primarily among God, in his more limited manifestations, the Son, and Adam and Eve, none of whom is as vulnerable to violence as are heroes who inherit original sin. Adam's loss of self-control and judgment after the fall is a sign of what will come later, as is Eve's interest in getting somewhere by working harder in the garden, or by eating the apple. Patience and heroic fortitude are the new epic virtues, and they are different, in Milton's mind, from self-control, because when well learned they do not require a holding back of unruly passion; they diminish its value as a temptation. But God, as we have seen, is capable of losing his self-control—more so, before the fall, than the other heroes of the poem.

Milton's subversion of human history is an effort to reorient his readers temporally so that they can see the worthlessness of worldly goals. As we have seen, this has required him to devalue not only the Royalist cause but the Puritan as well. The true heroism that is self-mastery and submission of oneself to life can be learned under any circumstances by a person who attends to inner rather than outer movements. When this is done, excessive violence should no longer occur since the hero will not have had to lose himself in a material cause for the sake of that cause. He will only have to stay in touch with life, which means, in Milton's terms, to pay attention to what God wants of him.

And he must, like other epic heroes before him, accept his mortality. God becomes conscious, creates, is confronted by opposition and death, and at once *takes on* death through the agency of the Son. The Son's offer to become mortal is no idle gesture. It is absolutely crucial and real, a permanent acceptance of mortality for the sake of life:

> Man disobeying,
> Disloyal breaks his fealtie, and sinns
> Against the high Supremacie of Heav'n,
> Affecting God-head, and so loosing all,
> To expiate his Treason hath naught left,
> But to destruction sacred and devote,
> He with his whole posteritie must dye,
> Dye hee or Justice must; unless for him

Som other able, and as willing, pay
The rigid satisfaction, death for death.
Say Heav'nly powers, where shall we find such love,
Which of ye will be mortal to redeem
Mans mortal crime, and just th'unjust to save,
Dwels in all Heaven charitie so deare?

[3.203–16]

The speech expresses no warmth, offers no mitigation. It
is typical of God's chilly rhetoric, and, as elsewhere, is
meant simply to express a fact of life, not to interpret it.
Life, creating itself, sees that it must again produce evil
and death, and draws back, asking itself whether it is equal
to the challenge. The Son, always life's best advocate, responds intensely in the affirmative, expressing his faith that
life can overcome death, bring good out of evil, triumph
in adversity. It is this loving faith which, being made one
with man's mortal nature, will prove redemptive. In his
next speech, God stresses the importance of the Son's taking on and keeping humanity:

. . . because in thee
Love hath abounded more then Glory abounds,
Therefore thy Humiliation shall exalt
With thee thy Manhood also to this Throne;
Here shalt thou sit incarnate, here shalt Reign
Both God and Man, Son both of God and Man,
Anointed universal King. . . .

[3.311–17]

Since God only creates through the agency of the Son,
the interchange is crucial. If life, then sin and death. If
death, then mortality. The Son himself has to encounter

death, and he does it unhesitatingly. That decision once made, it would seem that death could never again have the chance to veto life. The one *a priori* assumption that readers of *Paradise Lost* have to make is that life and creation are good, are worth it even in the face of death. More fully than their human creatures, God and the Son have already experienced the act of creation, and that experience gives them a strength of purpose that is perhaps not otherwise attainable. Of course, the poem is full of evidence of the wonder of creation; Book 7, especially, recovers for the reader the maker's joy. Nevertheless, every reader is vulnerable to Adam's, "Did I request thee, Maker, from my Clay / To mould me Man . . . ?" (10.743–44).

In fact, even the figure of God in Book 3 expresses life in conflict; the strife of mercy and justice, the presence of anger in God's face, are mentioned. The existence of Hell as a place of unwanted and unwelcome ideas has to be resolved. Part of what the Son has agreed to is to yield himself to the powers of darkness. Often, the ease with which the Son accepts Incarnation is given as evidence that he knows he will not really die. It is important not to take this way out. However one wants to understand the relationship between God and the Son—whether they are different characters or different aspects of the same character—the debate is real. The Son trusts to life to overcome death, but God has made no promises or interpretations, saying only that justice requires death. The Son concludes that by submitting himself unqualifiedly to death he can conquer it. Thus, he will lead Hell captive, the "powers of darkness bound," and replace the "cloud of anger" with reconciliation and peace. After the Son declares his intention and capacity to do these things, God predicts the fu-

ture and the restoration, or achievement, of wholeness at
the end of the world:

>   . . . all Power
> I give thee, reign for ever, and assume
> Thy Merits. . . .
>
> .   .   .   .
>
> The World shall burn, and from her ashes spring
> New Heav'n and Earth, wherein the just shall dwell,
> And after all thir tribulations long
> See golden days, fruitful of golden deeds,
> With Joy and Love triumphing, and fair Truth.
> Then thou thy regal Scepter shalt lay by,
> For regal Scepter then no more shall need,
> God shall be All in All. But all ye Gods,
> Adore him, who to compass all this dies,
> Adore the Son, and honour him as mee.
>
> [3.317–19, 334–43]

I have quoted so extensively from Book 3 because the language is crucial and difficult. Milton's God is not merely
enunciating a vengeful, outdated theology; he is expressing a chief means by which people individually and at all
times have learned to live. Given the necessary facts of
consciousness and death, one takes them on absolutely.
Given the fact that creation divides and alienates, one takes
on that knowledge, so that awareness of alienation can itself be used as a means toward wholeness.

God both does and does not give up his authority. As he
speaks for all life—past, present, and future—he cannot
simply abolish himself. He can at once repudiate whatever
aspect of himself was present in Satan. His capacity for
love, manifested in the Son and in the Son's power to confront Hell, to die and rise again, has enabled him to relin-

quish whatever sense he had of himself as static, a dictatorial king. That enables the Son's reconciling mission to be fulfilled.

The first humans were not intended to know death. The reason why they must—the power of death in the world—is the alienation occasioned by a greed that is often masked as curiosity. Desire for experience has been seen as an ambiguous epic goal, and when Satan sets forth to earth as a scout, he might seem little different from Odysseus or Guyon, or Vasco da Gama. But Satan's intention is different; he wants to know one thing only—how to turn earth into Hell—and he finds that out easily enough. Unlike da Gama's, his main purpose is conquest, and the first result of his journey is a Roman road paved from Hell through Chaos to the new territory.

Meeting Uriel, Satan disguises himself as a cherub, and claims to have come for the purpose of seeing and admiring God's works. The importance of virtuous motivation is apparent in Uriel's response:

> Fair Angel, thy desire which tends to know
> The works of God, thereby to glorifie
> The great Work-Maister, leads to no excess
> That reaches blame, but rather merits praise
> The more it seems excess, that led thee hither
> From thy Empyreal Mansion thus alone. . . .
>
> [3.694–99]

The desire to know, as Satan has expressed it, is not excessive because it neither distracts the supposed cherub from his function of praising God, nor is tainted by idle curiosity or by a desire to question the nature of things. It is simply expressed as an irresistible inner need to know and admire more fully God's creation in itself.

But Uriel is obviously concerned about excessive desire for knowledge. In *Paradise Lost,* Adam, the Son, and Satan are all compared to Prometheus. Both knowledge and experience, which may differ or coincide with one another, are ambiguous, risky. At her fall, Eve praises first knowledge, then experience, which she says opens wisdom's way. But what her experience has done is to alienate her from her own nature. Like all Milton's tempters, Satan has encouraged Eve to usurp herself, that is, to become godlike, as she already is. Before the fall, Adam and Eve have full experience of good, in the only way that it could be fully known, undiluted by experience of evil. The event of the fall requires a different kind of knowledge, not only to restore and strengthen vocation but to recover the self-knowledge that is lost.

In Dante's poem, Ulysses' desire for full experience wrecked his ship on the cliffs of Purgatory and sent him to the eighth circle of Hell. Ulysses' striving to know is something like what Adam manifests when he asks to have the solar system explained to him, and it seems laudable enough, as the impulse that brought men fire and language and many other things associated with human dignity. Even Christian tradition understands that, in a sense, the fall was fortunate, because it enabled poeple to experience Christ. But that concept balances on the edge of heresy.

Before the fall, Adam and Eve are already possessed of the treasures for which their descendants have to strive. They have warmth enough without dangerous fire. They have an exalted language. And they have the endlessly fulfilling garden that would be the ideal completion of quest in any postlapsarian age, though actually enjoyed only in Dante's poem. By his description of that garden as the fulfillment of all mythologies to come, without pain (the rose without thorn), yet wholly vulnerable to pain and degradation (we first see it through the eyes of its destroyer),[15] Milton conveys a postlapsarian sense of awe and excitement at life in Eden. Adam and Eve are in process, obviously learning their way, learning their relationship to each other, preparing for children. They are destined for spiritual striving toward the more fully conscious life of angels. Yet, although we can see all that, the accusation of boredom in Eden never entirely disappears, because that mode of being is unknown to us, because we are so much more sophisticated in worldly things than Adam and Eve, and because our own commitment is to a more familiar kind of striving. The task set for Adam and Eve is as perilous as any epic voyage—their fall shows that; its potential reward, in terms of spiritual growth, is more certain and complete. But the loss of Eden made western epic necessary, and western epic is what we know.

The fall resulted in man's restless commitment to striving, and to experience, sometimes for itself alone. The striving is always competitive, even when the person, like Ulysses, is only outpacing himself; it is always a mixed goodness. It is open, as Camoens' poem shows, to the alienating impulses of imperialism, greed, objectification. Ulysses is detached from his spiritual center. Eve's first thought is to keep the apple from Adam, so as to gain some superiority over him, and she only changes her mind for fear that she will die and he will find another Eve. Hard on the heels of da Gama comes the Portuguese empire. It would have been better to let body work up to spirit, according to the original plan.

Adam wants to understand the universe before he has

begun to understand his relationship with his wife. He has
put Eve on a pedestal, objectifying her, not allowing her
humanity. He thinks he knows all about domestic life, but
what he knows he has learned from Renaissance books—
that Eve, like a good wife, should have a storeroom full
of food, for instance, when it is obvious that things do not
work that way in Paradise. This unfunctional curiosity
Renaissance scholars called *scientia* without *conscientia*,[16]
and it is what Satan evokes when he calls the Tree the
mother of science (9.680). In splitting off from God, in
making and adumbrating scientific discoveries (gunpowder,
evolution, and so forth) that both increase human domination and cause alienation, in preferring his own isolated
ego to immersion in any kind of whole, Satan illustrates
both the fall of man and the course of modern civilization.

Experience of this sort is opposed to self-knowledge of
the kind that God intended for Adam and Eve in their
creation:

> There wanted yet the Master work, the end
> Of all yet don; a Creature who not prone
> And Brute as other Creatures, but endu'd
> With Sanctitie of Reason, might erect
> His Stature, and upright with Front serene
> Govern the rest, self-knowing, and from thence
> Magnanimous to correspond with Heav'n,
> But grateful to acknowledge whence his good
> Descends, thither with heart and voice and eyes
> Directed in Devotion, to adore
> And worship God Supream, who made him chief
> Of all his works. . . .
>
> [7.505–16]

And early in Book 10, God scolds Adam's neglect of himself for Eve:

> . . . her Gifts
> Were such as under Government well seem'd,
> Unseemly to beare rule, which was thy part
> And person, had'st thou known thy self aright.
> [10.153–56]

Self-knowledge before the Renaissance meant knowing one's place in life, one's role or person. It meant, most of all, knowing God and living in relationship with God. It was the opposite of self-consciousness because it kept the emphasis on relationship based on unity. And it could not have included the desire for experience because that desire opposes the individual ego to the given community.

In fact, Milton's use of the word "self-knowing" is the earliest given in the *OED*. Whatever philosophers may have discussed in Latin, ordinary medieval Englishmen never thought about knowing themselves; they did not have to. And if Milton's is one of the first uses of the word in English, it may also be one of the last to signify the human being's easy integrity with the world. For, as soon as a person becomes aware of knowing himself as a separate and distinct part of life, he loses the capacity to be unself-conscious.

I have mentioned before the common idea that the fall of man into self-consciousness happened in the Renaissance. People had defined themselves within medieval contexts and patterns which now were breaking up. With the printing press and gunpowder, they acquired mass means of self-knowledge and self-destruction, the powers of tech-

nology and alienation, and, with varying degrees of awareness, they knew it. *Paradise Lost* officially records this
moment, knows itself to be an alienated poem, and so becomes, in more sweeping historical terms than we have yet
considered, the epic of its age.[17]

It is self-consciousness, not self-knowledge in the old
sense, that brings about awareness of death. Adam's and
Eve's lack of self-consciousness is what makes modern
readers scornful of them, yet that is just what enables the
self-knowledge of their unity with life. Even the sexual
distinctions are intended as illustration of unself-conscious
roles. Yet, just here, the poem finds humanity vulnerable.
Adam at his creation is already aware of his limitedness,
of his need for completion in another. And in order to
achieve relationship with Adam, Eve has to be consciously
taken from her natural affinity to earth and water, and
taught to admire a lover whom she at first finds unattrac-
tive. Perhaps even the insistence that Adam should know
himself is self-defeating: we are returned to the recognition that creation in itself requires opposition and implies
evil. At least that seems to be true of creation since the
Renaissance.

Stanley Fish's thesis in *Surprised by Sin* is that Milton's
intention was to make the reader fall in the poem, so as to
enable him not to fall in reality.[18] But what we see is a
more difficult and more Christian acknowledgment. The
nature of creation is to be fallen, to be divided, and, in
dividedness, to long for unity. The hermaphroditic ideal
that some philosophers have posited was not Adam's.
Without objectification of male and female, Adam could
not hold with himself the fit conversation that Milton

thought of as the definition of marriage. In the failure of that conversation both partners lost themselves.

Like Adam, Eve is beguiled by the idea of gaining knowledge and experience beyond what she already has. The serpent persuades her that the Tree will raise her as it had already raised him; after she eats the fruit, her first thoughts are in praise of sapience, wisdom, and experience. When the temporary intoxication has passed, the human couple take refuge in the woods. Still physically in Paradise, they are already in the cave; God's words, "Where art thou *Adam*" (10.103), are a request for a spiritual accounting, in response to which they express their eagerness to deceive themselves and God by blaming each other and the serpent. Then with the garden changed and concealment unavailing, they consider suicide. This is the moment of humanity's greatness in this epic, although at first it does not appear so. They have to take the responsibility of assuming mortality not only for themselves but for the whole human race. Faith in their own damaged relationships with each other and with God enables them to become heroic.

It is hard for them to give up the physical reality of Paradise, but the point of making them do so is to demonstrate that there is no such physical reality, for human beings, any more. In the Flood, that will be further emphasized when Eden is washed away to become a barren island. The false paradise that is located on the outside of earth nearest to Heaven is first visited by Satan on his way to Eden. This place, which in Milton's time will be "to few unknown," promises reward to all who put their trust in earthly things:

              . . . all who in vain things
    Built thir fond hopes of Glorie or lasting fame,
    Or happiness in this or th'other life;
    All who have thir reward on Earth, the fruits
    Of painful Superstition and blind Zeal. . . .
                                    [3.448–52]

The scene in Hell where the fallen angels uselessly gorge themselves on ashen apples might also be considered a satiric version of Paradise. Other epics made their false Edens extremely attractive. Milton surrounds those attractive traps, on the one hand, with the real thing explicitly compared to the later imitations, and, on the other hand, with these grotesque parodies. What enables Adam and Eve to reject the idea of suicide, despite their loss of Eden, is essentially a desire to participate in the plan of creation. Because they are able to put aside the original impulses, first toward self-gratification, and later toward despair, they win the promise Michael gives them of "a paradise within thee, happier farr" (12.587). And with that, Paradise, like Hell, has become a state of mind.

In the first part of this essay, I discussed the paradoxical isolation of the hero in relation to the communal enterprise of which he is a part. In his solitude, he changes human consciousness. In this poem, God, the Son, and Adam and Eve serve to explain the isolation that overtakes humanity. God, although he has solitude, is not isolated, because he exists in communion with the Son. That kind of perfect mirroring is what human beings are supposed to enjoy. But Adam and Eve are born out of harmony; they do not have intuitive understanding of each other as God and the angels do, and their differences from each other do not always please them. Milton shapes his poems as much as other writers to the ideal of an harmonious nation or community. But, as much as they, he sees that ideal almost impossible to achieve, even in a community of two. Adam and Eve allow their spiritual differences to separate them. God becomes himself through creation, and in his solitude he creates living things who will come to participate in him. Adam and Eve separately make a choice that endows the human race with original sin, and another that allows them to have another chance. All these actions involve changes in consciousness, as well as the creation of consciousness itself.

In the solitude of their journeys into consciousness, some epic heroes are at times unlikable; so, in similar yet opposing ways, are God, and Adam and Eve. God appears too officious and remote, and Adam and Eve too limitedly perfect to be human. God gives Adam and Eve a pattern of his own consciousness, but diminished, and divided between them. Adam's and Eve's desire for experience, and Adam's desire for his wife, both potentially sinful, have seemed to many readers their most sympathetic attributes. They both diminish and increase human consciousness. Their fall itself makes it hard for their descendants to appreciate prelapsarian persons: the heirs of original sin prefer experience to innocence. Beatrice's ironic question to Dante, "Why are you here? Don't you know that here men are happy?" could also be the motto of *Paradise Lost*. Because Satan, and Adam and Eve, rebelled against happiness, epic heroes ever since have had to hunt for it without a chance of finding it permanently in this life.

Yet occasionally, as in previous epics, there is a hint of fulfillment. Milton characteristically uses typology to unify history's patterns and show how any person can at-

tach himself to the pattern of eternity. The meeting between the Son and Adam and Eve after the fall is extraordinary for its multileveled intensity. God judges the fallen
pair, but he also clothes them in anticipation of their meeting again, when Christ bathes the feet of his disciples.
Then in this scene both God and Adam represent Christ as
second Adam, and Eve prefigures Mary. The fusion of
God with flesh is already real in this moment that also
promises the reality of eternity in time, collapsing fall and
redemption into a single act. The act itself is loving and
spontaneous, but it occurs in a scene that is intensely Biblical, ritualized:

> So judg'd he Man, both Judge and Saviour sent,
> And th'instant stroke of Death denounc't that day
> Remov'd farr off; then pittying how they stood
> Before him naked to the aire, that now
> Must suffer change, disdain'd not to begin
> Thenceforth the form of servant to assume,
> As when he wash'd his servants feet so now
> As Father of his Familie he clad
> Thir nakedness with Skins of Beasts. . . .
>
> [10.209–17]

In its Old Testament context, Milton's original use of the
scene as type of a New Testament action is impressive.
History is both chosen and fulfilled.

Another way in which Milton suggests fulfillment in
time is to show God moving from transcendence toward
immanence during the course of the poem. Paradise and
Hell move within; the soul is the image of God in man;
man will no longer be able to talk to God in the garden.
That this shift has both advantages and drawbacks should
be apparent in history as well as in this poem. Satan is the

archetypal example of a person who listens only to himself; his version of immanent godhood is his own perverse will. Man's sense of his ability to create and recreate himself is challenging, and has enabled communities to be inspired with common purpose. But it also has contributed to human divisiveness and to the sensitive, isolated egotism of contemporary selfhood.

Throughout this study it should seem apparent that Milton has moved God and humanity closer together than, in the epic, they have ever been before. God is losing some of his transcendence, and his freedom from the constraints and limitations of history; but humanity has twice been raised to godlike stature, first in the creation, and second in the Incarnation. The fact of God's involvement in history makes human beings freer of it than ever before, each person able to find his epiphanic time without being as responsible as before to make use of the actual historical circumstances of his life. Both God and Adam and Eve, because they are not limited to history, are entirely committed to self-fulfillment, which is their life together, in its movement toward a time when God will be all in all. Death has to be accepted; at the same time, the hero's (any person's) godlike yearnings can be fulfilled because God himself has accepted death.

Milton, like Shakespeare, precisely identifies the problems that beset our own age. Shakespeare offered no solution other than a reaffirmation of medieval values that had come to be taken, and scorned, by rote. Perhaps this is also true of Milton; certainly for those to whom words like "eternity" and "transcendence" have become meaningless, there can be little belief in paradise within. But he uses the same tools with which epic has traditionally delineated the

achievement, use, and transcendence of self-consciousness—
the emphasis on art within art, mirroring, pairs, and opposites. And he offers, as we have seen, the hope that these
opposites occur in order that a higher synthesis may be
sought.

At one end of the range, devices of art and mirroring attach to Satan and his forces—traditional epic tools now
used to mock and undermine. To while away the time
while their leader is gone, the fallen angels sing their exploits, and engage in the traditional funeral games which,
in this instance, signify their spiritual death. Leaving Hell,
Satan is stopped by Sin and Death, his daughter-lover and
son, creatures who reflect him absolutely and whom he fails
to recognize until told who they are. Then he reaffirms
his love for his own. The epic shield ordinarily is a work
of art that carries important information about the heroic
task. But Satan's shield

> Hung on his shoulders like the Moon, whose Orb
> Through Optic Glass the *Tuscan* Artist views
> At Ev'ning from the top of *Fesole*,
> Or in *Valdarno*, to descry new Lands,
> Rivers or Mountains in her spotty Globe.
>
> [1.287–91]

Satan's shield is like the moon as seen through the tele-
scope of Galileo as he searches out new lands. This complex simile serves to distance and diminish Satan, making
him seem acted upon rather than acting; it equates him
with the instability and uncertainty of the moon; it connects him with modern science and technology; and it
indirectly casts some discredit upon modern science by
sliding Satan together with the moon as the object of its

inquiries. Certainly Milton did not intend altogether to condemn Galileo, whom he admired, and who he thought had been overly condemned already, but to the extent that moon-gazing represents curiosity, he discredits it. In each of these instances, the art-within-art connected with Satan seemingly reminds us of epic quest, creation, and discovery, but repeatedly affirms that such questing leads to ignorance, self-destruction, and death. This is no hostility to modernity, but Milton saw more clearly than most the dangers that ride with humanism, and his intention is to rescue it from itself.

At the opposite pole from Satanic art-within-art are the two angelic narratives by Raphael and Michael. Their extensive presence devotes almost half the poem to what might well be thought of as university lectures, although they are so absorbing (especially Raphael's) that few readers ever consider this fact. The equivalent in earlier epic is not the much more businesslike visitation of the heavenly messengers, but the narration by epic heroes of their own adventures, the device enabling the poem to start in the midst of things. Adam was meant to learn about epic heroism by hearing how it was handled by God and Satan. His own heroism was to consist simply in spiritual growth and in resistance to temptation, in behavior finally achieved on his behalf by Christ.

Raphael's stories include everything that Adam and Eve need to know about life, but their focus is creation and destruction. In response to all this, Adam tells the story of his own creation, and Eve's. The art of Raphael and Adam is mutually reflective, and has art for its subject. The function of art as Milton understood it in 1660 is to minister to a fallen and self-conscious world. But Adam and Eve

unself-consciously are what postlapsarian art tries to recover. All that they do is art: their work in the garden
(which consists of pruning), their cadenced prayers, the
garland Adam makes for Eve, even the way they walk and
move together. These perfect acts illustrate the dictionary
definition of art as "the making or doing of things that
have form and beauty." Adam and Eve are among God's
highest, riskiest creations; in expressing themselves, they
express him. In falling, they mar themselves and his work.

Before the fall, they were not lacking in self-consciousness. Adam's account of his relationship with Eve, and
Eve's effort to spend some time alone, are both self-
conscious acts. But generally speaking, that kind of behavior is postlapsarian. Before the fall, conscious art was
primarily the domain of God and Satan. The riskiness of
art, its connection with death and evil, was God's discovery. While Adam and Eve exist in the garden, their art is
flawless, and can never be as interesting to us as ours, because it is uncolored by mortality.

The same could be true of the art of Heaven. Choruses
of alleluias tend to bear out human suspicions about the
monotony of celestial existence. However, when the poet
himself joins his voice with those of the angels, he un-
expectedly brings all Heaven to our ears and teases us into
attending to that mortal note. The reflexiveness—the response of song to song—which has constantly to be achieved
on earth is a natural condition of existence there, as evidenced first of all in the invocation to light-fountain-stream
at the beginning of Book 3. In the *Paradiso*, Dante shows
the process by which, at the highest pitch of their being,
all creatures, while remaining distinctive in themselves,
reflect each other. That phenomenon is exemplified in

Paradise Lost, especially in Adam and Eve, and the Father and Son, and parodied in Satan and Beelzebub. God and the Son are two aspects of the same being; they enlighten, express, and magnify each other:

> Beyond compare the Son of God was seen
> Most glorious, in him all his Father shon
> Substantially express'd, and in his face
> Divine compassion visibly appeerd,
> Love without end, and without measure Grace,
> Which uttering thus he to his Father spake.
>   O Father, gracious was that word which clos'd
> Thy sovran sentence, that Man should find grace. . . .
>
> [3.138–45]

This complete mutuality, expressed in mirroring language, is for both Dante and Milton the aim of creation, an aspiration shown in a more worldly fashion in the embrace with which epic typically concludes. Man is "in unity defective," requires a mate, yet two-ness breeds disharmony and difficult matchings on the way to higher union. It is presumed, also, that there is a stage beyond this one, when God is all in all, and language as we know it must cease. To enter the kingdom of Heaven is to lose the need for symbols and signs, and the art of Heaven is not so boring as it is superfluous.

Don Parry Norford has described the poem partly in terms of the coincidence of opposites;[19] his argument is that evil is God's means to action. Without Satan, all things would remain forever in stasis; therefore God provokes evil to come into being. God and Satan do obviously belong to an archetypal pattern of creativeness, and between them they bring Adam into the state of self-consciousness that for us is human. But Milton never portrays God and

Satan as a pair. God's own capacity for darkness has already been considered; he is himself the origin of pairs, a coincidence of opposites, and Satan is the risk God takes in realizing opposition in creation. However, the great patterns of opposition and mutual reflection—day and night, sun and moon, male and female—certainly are intrinsic to the poem.

In fact, almost everything in *Paradise Lost* can be seen as a gathering in of opposites, twins, mutually reflective characters, symbols, and stories. To some extent, God and the Son set off the Old Testament against the New, and we have already seen what resonance Milton can achieve by typological means. The poem also harmonizes classical with Christian myth by constantly describing the events and characters of Genesis in terms of their supposed mythological descendants. To take a very simple example, Milton concludes his initial description of Adam and Eve in this way:

> So hand in hand they passd, the lovliest pair
> That ever since in loves imbraces met,
> *Adam* the goodliest man of men since borne
> His Sons, the fairest of her Daughters *Eve*.
>
> [4.321–24]

And in the description of Eden just preceding, there has been mention of Proserpine gathering flowers, a foreshadowing of the fall, before Adam and Eve are even introduced. Milton evokes in Adam and Eve their own descendants as imperfect twins, and foreshadows the fall by mirroring it in a supposedly later myth. By these means Milton both distinguishes and unifies in the same way that Dante does, but on a much vaster scale. The incipient exis-

tence of everything in everything else makes eternity a
reality in the texture of the poem.

With the downplaying of physical quest, guest-friendship
becomes less important in Milton's poem. Raphael's visit
to Adam and Eve may be so considered; as described already, it is a visit of mutual interest and profit. It also, of
course, fits the category of heavenly messenger. The visits
of God and Michael to the garden cannot very usefully be
described here, since there is so little of the traditional
mode, in which the hero is the visitor, and host and guest
are wary of each other.

The relationship between male and female, however, is
obviously central. Upon being created, Adam rejected sin-
gleness, and God rejected it for him. Androgyny is not
elected by the Bible to represent man's original state. Milton makes Adam ask God for an equal, and the two of
them are first described thus:

> Two of far nobler shape erect and tall,
> Godlike erect, with native Honour clad
> In naked Majestie seemd Lords of all,
> And worthie seemd, for in thir looks Divine
> The image of thir glorious Maker shon,
> Truth, wisdome, Sanctitude severe and pure. . . .
>
> [4.288–93]

Both reflect God, and each reflects the other. With the actual working out of the marriage, however, still another
kind of vision comes into being, more along the lines of
Don Parry Norford's argument. Eve is associated with nature and the imagination, Adam with air and sky and reason. In neither one is the dominant quality very adequately
developed. The two people are dependent on one another

for fulfillment of these different faculties. Separated from Adam, Eve lets her imagination give way to fancy; separated from Eve, Adam lets his reasoning lead him to despair.

Eve probably tends to see herself as more self-sufficient than she really is: her initial desire to look at herself in the water is a traditional image of the contemplative soul, but also of course of narcissism, and, cut off as it is, remains ambiguous. Adam relates to Eve as would any hero of romance epic, but his Neoplatonism goes wrong, and he worships her blindly, seeing her as absolute in herself, superior to authority and reason, and thus reinforcing her instinctive tendency toward self-sufficiency. Their portrayal is as interesting a critique of traditional attitudes as anything in Spenser, as well as a psychologically sophisticated portrayal of the marriage.

Milton associates Eve with the "darkness" of the unconscious and the creative powers, that is, a darkness capable of producing both good and evil, but essential to creativity. Thus she can symbolize the risk inherent in the creative process, but, for that matter, so can Adam. Milton understands and accepts that risk without fear; it is a purpose of the whole poem to tell us so. Both before and after the fall, Adam can find no reason to want to live without Eve. They ruin one another, but it is Eve who first is able to begin the restorative process. Their recovery then is only less spectacular than the fact that Milton is able to make it believable. We seem to accept unquestioningly that total reaffirmation of one another which, if we thought about it in "real life" terms, would seem miraculous. We see them respond to their intuitive knowledge of one another, cease to think of one another as adversaries, believably create a new myth of oneness, a happier Paradise, as they leave Paradise hand in hand.

Their holding hands is a motif in the poem,[20] indicating their inseparability. If Adam could not be made androgynous, the path of humanity may lead toward androgyny, even as the course of all things is toward a higher unity. When Adam asks Raphael about sex in Heaven, Raphael says that heavenly sex is superior (8.620–29). Elsewhere it has been said that angels can assume either sex or both (1.423–24). And they can merge totally with one another. Since Adam and Eve were intended to achieve the state of angels, one can assume that androgyny is an aspect of that perfect unity toward which the whole creation moves.

Another indication of that unity is the ambiguous sex of Milton's muse, which some scholars have identified with the Son.[21] In some places called "she," in others "he," identified variously with Urania, the Son, the Spirit, and God, the traditionally feminine source of inspiration is not a woman on a pedestal but a creative drive that incorporates and transcends both sexes. Milton has been called a sexist, although his attitude toward women is unusually advanced for his time. Certainly in these indications of a desire to move beyond sexual opposites, he is far ahead of most of his contemporaries. The poem's world is in transition: even its most unsympathetic reflections of complements and opposites try, in their contexts, to engage us in a dialectic that reminds us repeatedly of the extent to which Milton's culture is also ours.

Reflective twinning is as prevalent in *Paradise Lost* as elsewhere in the tradition, and is of course intrinsic to the thematic coincidence of opposites. As in Spenser, there are numerous look-alikes, of which the most important is the endless parodying of God and Heaven by Satan and Hell. As everyone knows, Satan takes on a series of disguises, beginning with the practically impenetrable disguise of cherub and progressing through increasingly degenerated and uncontrollable forms to his final metamorphosis into the serpent who compulsively eats the apples of death.

One kind of reflection that Milton has done superbly in most of his poetry is falsely reflective reasoning. He always allows his villains more apparently persuasive arguments than his heroes have, a more sensuously compelling style. Their arguments parody his own beliefs in regard to the proper use of things of this world. In particular, they hold up to those tempted their own vocations, urging them to become what they are. Thus Eve is offered wisdom, knowledge of good and evil, and a godlike state, all of which she has in the best sense, though not in the sense Satan intends. By eating the apple, she loses wisdom, gains experience of evil, loses innocent knowledge of good and evil, and loses her godlike condition. The tempter's arguments are persuasive because they speak to what the person already is, but they intend a debased, "worldly" version of it. They prey on self-ignorance and self-forgetfulness. The simple enough remedy is awareness of self in one's own context, that is to say, knowledge of self in God. Eve had that, but Adam's idolatry combined with her own willful curiosity had put her off.

After the fall, when Michael reveals history to Adam, he has lost the power to distinguish right from wrong and has to be re-educated. Setting happy looks against sad ones, Adam concludes that good cheer goes with good and sadness with evil. Michael has to teach him to pay attention to vocation and spiritual context, not to appearances of worldly prosperity. However, sensory knowledge is not untrustworthy in Milton to the extent that it is in Ariosto and perhaps in Spenser. Hypocrisy, as in Spenser, can go undetected. But Milton is more admiring of an authentic life of the senses than any epic poet since Homer. The simple majesty of the figures of Adam and Eve, the description of the garden, the praise of sex in marriage as beautiful in itself (rather than, as is more usual, justified with a flourish of genealogy charts) all testify to this fact.

Milton also works interestingly with the relationship between earth and Heaven. From Satan's point of view, Heaven is not knowable, for to an entirely materialistic mind the vocabularies of earth do not include the concept of Heaven. Although physically invulnerable to death, he has to live and achieve entirely in a world of time without reference to eternity, and he entices Adam and Eve to do the same. On the other hand, the acceptance of the existence of eternity calls forth a sense of the spiritual dimension of life that devulgarizes material things. This, I think, accounts for some of the apparent contradictions in Raphael. He is a spirit, yet he feels hunger and shares a meal with Adam and Eve. It is explained that lower things constantly feed higher, are transformed into higher: the use that is made of anything helps to determine its nature.

Raphael repeats that it is difficult to explain anything that goes on in Heaven, and at once asks an unanswered question implying it may not be difficult at all:

> . . . how last unfould
> The secrets of another world, perhaps
> Not lawful to reveal? yet for thy good

This is dispenc't, and what surmounts the reach
Of human sense, I shall delineate so,
By lik'ning spiritual to corporal forms,
As may express them best, though what if Earth
Be but the shadow of Heav'n, and things therein
Each to other like, more then on earth is thought?

[5.568–76]

If Raphael does not know the answer to this question, one might ask, who does? Just as God is expressed in the Son because the Son is able by merit to give himself up to God, earth and Heaven will express each other badly or well depending on the quality of their mutuality. Everything is in process, nothing fixed. Everything reflects everything else, and at best earth is already Paradise, as Dante also meant his poem to show.

The relationship between fathers and sons is a dominant theme in *Paradise Lost,* to an extent that has not been true of most Christian epics. God cannot be outgrown or transcended; that would be a contradiction in terms. What we see instead is that he constantly outgrows and transcends himself, finds new ways to express himself, always having the opportunity to create new worlds. The children of life can choose how much participation in the process they want, and Satan chooses none. The Son wants it all, expresses his father fully, and so God gives up lordship to him, a means by which life transcends itself and which (as Milton will show more fully in *Paradise Regained*) is available to all people.

The war in Heaven cannot be won or lost finally because it is a war between life and death, which is never-ending. God can make a demonstration, showing that life cannot be killed, and does that in sending out the Son to put Heaven back in order, and frighten the fallen angels into Hell. In choosing opposition to life, Satan has given birth to Death, his son, who expresses and limits him perfectly, for he must believe himself immortal and at the same time must love and seek to express himself only through death. That choice between life and death is what Adam and Eve have too, more simply before the fall than afterwards. At every given moment before history and in it, they and their descendants are reaffirming an alliance, choosing to be sons and daughters of life or death, and choosing it for their descendants as well. I have already made reference to that key moment in the poem when God, the Son, Adam, and Eve all become simultaneously each other's parent and child. For while, in one sense, everything is lost, in another nothing ever is. Life as parent is not that which is discarded, but that which is constantly reborn or renewed, the youngest child of the human race as well as its revolutionary begetter.

The poet is present in *Paradise Lost*, and is surely one of its heroes. In its powerful prefaces he examines and accepts his own mortality, as particularly evidenced in his blindness, the dangers by which he is surrounded, and the possibility that the poem itself may be an empty dream. Nevertheless, he undertakes the epic flight, claims that the poem is not just brought to him, but that he participates in its experience, descends to Hell, and returns:

> Taught by the heav'nly Muse to venture down
> The dark descent, and up to reascend,
> Though hard and rare. . . .
>
> [3.19–21]

Twice he uses the word "safe" to describe his return, here where he reascends from Hell, and again in Book 7:

> Standing on Earth, not rapt above the Pole,
> More safe I Sing with mortal voice, unchang'd
> To hoarce or mute. . . .
>
> [7.23–25]

Despite the perils of his physical surroundings, in the early days of the Restoration when his life was politically threatened, Milton reminds us of Dante in his assertion of the greater danger of the spiritual voyage. William Riggs argues that the poet defines himself as hero in the poem by a series of comparisons of himself with other characters,[22] and I should like simply to summarize that thesis here. The intentional paralleling of Satan's presumptuousness with the poet's clearly distinguishes Satan's insistence on self-sufficiency from the poet's reliance on God's inspiration. Adam and Eve, like the poet, thirst for knowledge, but where Adam and Eve both seek knowledge for its own sake, Milton aims to assert eternal providence. Like the angels, Milton needs and finds heavenly light to explain God's ways to men. Raphael and Michael demonstrate in their narratives some of the limitations and range of Christian poetry. Finally, the Son, like the poet, is seen as a medium through whom the Father shines, and both Son and poet are led in their creative tasks by the Spirit-muse. Always aware of the solitude and danger of his enterprise, the poet proves himself the true Christian by taking on these extraordinary confrontations in order to test his belief that he is about God's business, not Satan's, that the temple of *Paradise Lost,* neither Pandemonium nor Solomon's, is the "upright heart and pure."

In addition to these conscious checks upon himself, the poet's heroism certainly consists centrally in the fact that he is a prophet writing an inspired work whose intention is to justify God's ways to men.[23] This was the danger and the complexity of the task: it required Milton to write a poem that was a course in a theology only partially familiar to his time. He had to do it blind, unable to see where he had been or where he was going, holding it all in his mind as it came to him, relying on others to spell and punctuate correctly, and relying on God to let the poem speak to a world that had already rejected the politics of his vision. The patience and heroic fortitude that for him had come to define heroism apply absolutely to the story of the making of this work.

Milton called out of the epic its own ambivalences, and faced them more directly than had been done before, while at the same time adding new imponderables of his own. John Steadman mentions Milton's unfairness to the tradition as a typically revolutionary attitude: the genre was not as fond of "long and tedious havoc" as Milton pretended.[24] It was simply that when this seemed to be the mode of procedure, the hero worked out his salvation in battle or not at all: Achilles shows this necessity more clearly than any of his successors. In Christian epic, however, both the classical apparatus and the warfare had become somewhat of an embarrassment, some poets transforming their material more successfully than others. Few readers are impressed by Camoens' double set of deities. Ariosto simply does not take deity or warfare seriously. In Tasso, although the discrepancy between Christian ideal and epic reality is intolerable, that tension itself is used as a part of the poem's esthetics, since the poet found nowhere else to go. By allegorizing his poem, and focusing his exploration on love, Spenser was able successfully to challenge some central epic assumptions about love and war, and to make the giving up of some of the classical apparatus intrinsic to his story without jarring it. Spenser's insistence on an artificial continuity with an almost nonexistent English literary tradition makes what now seem unnecessarily great demands upon the modern reader, but within its own world the poem works brilliantly.

With Calepine's discovery in Book 6 of the *Faerie Queene* that he can run faster without armor, Spenser concludes a series of reappraisals of the epic ideal that, together with Dante's earlier explicit spiritualization of the genre, paves the way for Milton. Milton's central task, in *Paradise Lost*, required him to be more boldly theological than any of his predecessors, discarding the classical gods as figures in their own right, asserting his role as prophet, and allowing himself to be the vehicle of a new description of the ways of God to men. If we have had no further great epics, it is not because Milton ended the tradition, but because we are still living out the myth that Milton helped to renew.

Of course Milton borrows in all kinds of ways from his predecessors, as has been amply shown in other scholarship. His debt to Homer has not been sufficiently recognized, probably because a mistaken idea of Milton's Latinity has been so ingrained in us. The particular majesty of the style of *Paradise Lost*, the sculptured simplicity of the characters of Adam and Eve, the sharing of heroism among several different kinds of characters, are all quite distinctively Homeric and will so affect anyone coming to *Paradise Lost* directly from a steady reading through the other epics. Vergil, on the other hand, is his major primary source for the antiheroic, both in the stern and pious heroism of Aeneas and in the more negative though sympathetic figure of Turnus. Vergil's undermining of the Augustan ideal is, together with all epic underminings, a pattern for Milton. Dante is his most important spiritual predecessor, but he learned and borrowed from them all.

Although Milton's use of the Bible cannot, except implicitly, be a subject of this study, it would not be appropriate to ignore it in discussion of his reworking of tradition. A definition of Milton's achievement is its combination into one poem of all that was most important to him in the classical and in the Judaeo-Christian heritage. Renaissance readers thought of the Bible as an epic; he made it one in fact.[25] God looks through the eyes of Zeus; the epic begins with Genesis and ends with Revelation, in the most extensive and successful mirror-imaging yet attempted.[26]

Like other epic poems, Milton's begins in the middle of things, and reflects upon itself, stories like the creation and the war in heaven being told and retold from different points of view. In its historical perspective, as I have already mentioned, it has a unique advantage. Although it is the last to be written in this series of epics, its fiction is that the action contained in it is the first to occur and yet contains all the others. Thus, Milton had all history and all literary history available to him; biblical typology and Christian humanism helped to show him how to deal with it. As ambitious as anything that any Renaissance overreacher ever undertook, it has the triumph of being a whole and finished poem at the same time that, even in its title, it calls out for more.

We could see in the poem and its publishing history

signs of its problematic and open character even if we knew little or nothing of Milton's biography. Aside from other evidence of his decision about what the subject of the epic should be and the many years of its incubation, he tells us in Book 9 of his "long choosing, and beginning late," the lateness of the age, the inadequacy of the models, the cold climate, his own age, and the unpopular vision that may prevent success. It was first published under the initials J.M., by a nervous printer who gave it six different title pages during the sale of the first edition, and farmed it out to six different booksellers. Milton's name was not considered to be much of an advantage. But Restoration readers bought the book, and within seven months had apparently caused Milton to include in it an aggressive explanation of "why the poem rimes not." On his own behalf, he was thinking about why the poem had ten books; they became twelve in the second edition, published in 1674, the year of his death.

Although Milton is notorious for his so-called passive heroes, the main characters of the poem are all busy doing something; they are in process. God (through the Son) makes all creation; the angels fight a war and Satan's forces establish an empire; Satan falls to Hell, rallies his troops, makes the trip to earth, seduces Eve, and flies back; Adam and Eve are born, learn what they are to aim for, fall, recover themseves, and leave Paradise; the Son concludes the war in Heaven, comes to earth to judge and mediate, and returns to Heaven. And although these are the main events, the poem is made a container for the whole Bible, which itself contains everything past, passing, and to come. Yet even though we also have the nonchronology of eternity to contend with, the story line is easy to follow, much easier than those of Ariosto and Spenser. It may be, in fact, that in the original version Milton thought the story too evident. The revision emphasizes the non-narrative pattern in the books of destruction and creation, as Books 6 and 7, at the center of the poem, thus allowing all the resonantly patterned language of that eternal opposition—stand-fall, for example—to radiate outward from those books.

In other epics, the nonnarrative pattern allows the reader to reintegrate the apparent opposites of action and contemplation, although the story itself is not just an account of progress toward a goal, and the pattern itself is not static. These things are also true of *Paradise Lost*. But in this poem the characters are literally both the immediate source and the result of activity and pattern. We see in God the beginning and the end of action, the ceaseless motion of eternity, and in Satan the false action of degenerate quest, the false contemplation of Hell's philosophy and song. And the poem contains the pattern for all future transcendent moments, in the meeting of God and Adam in the garden.

Consideration of the epic embrace in *Paradise Lost* requires a final look at the relationship between God and Satan. In every other epic, opposing principles come to terms with each other; God and Satan do not, and at first it would seem that any attempt to justify this difference would have to be a rationalization. Yet there is an essential difference, despite the obvious important likeness. God himself contains warring elements, opposing principles from which darkness and the possibility of evil have come. To exile and eventually to dissolve Satan is not to reject opposition, only that aspect of opposition which is finally and entirely hostile to life. Although we have seen that Satan is in some sense useful to existence, he is useful only as an idea, a negative pole, and not in himself a vital force. In every other epic, the two opposite embracing forces have been the archetypal forms of light and dark, masculine and feminine, civilized and wild, rational and intuitive, and so forth. These opposite forms all exist within God, but that countering force is not exemplified in Satan, who is finally the nullification of all action and form. Everything that Satan does diminishes him. The same is not true of the greatest counterforces of earlier epic. Achilles at the end is stronger than Priam. Turnus understands and accepts his destiny in an affirmative way, and is as necessary as Aeneas to the character of Rome. Energy and femininity are practically inseparable from one another in such characters, and in many of the poems the countervailing force is literally feminine, Penelope and Beatrice being the great examples. But, again, God contains in himself both masculine and feminine and in himself is beyond both. Although there is a sort of sympathy between Satan and Eve, there is nothing feminine about Satan himself, or masculine either; he is more like a eunuch, and his coupling with Sin is a perpetual, frustrating act of narcissism.

While Satan's role in relation to God does resemble that of other great oppositions in that Satan is used to bring about wholeness, there are in the poem more essential sets of opposites at work. Satan is a byproduct, a tool, and a symbol of sterility and nothingness, as shown by the self-embrace in which he is literally transformed into a hissing serpent (10.511–14). The essential oppositions are the darkness within God himself, part of which (the finally dispensable part) is identifiable with Satan, and the warring elements of Chaos. The union that is to come at the end of the world is occasionally foreshadowed in human life, in the embraces that take place in the conclusions of epic, and in the great moments of transcendence which, occurring anywhere within the poem, indicate that we are not merely talking about chronological time. The reconciliation and hand-in-handedness of Adam and Eve at the end of the poem is the obvious typical epic embrace in *Paradise Lost*. Like those of Achilles and Priam, their powers have destroyed each other, then sought out reaffirmation and renewal on a different level than before. *Paradise Lost* ends with a new beginning. The world is all before Adam and Eve, as it is all before Odysseus: theirs is the first epic story to accept absolutely the joint necessity and active heroism of male and female. Spenser accepts it, but his poem is still dominated by the actions of male heroes. The difference comes about partly because what women have always stood for, the apparent passivity of their patience and heroic fortitude, has become for Milton an essential attribute of the hero. The feminine principle, necessary to creation, is also necessary to the acceptance of mortality and the continuation of life.

Another important embrace in this epic is the return of the Son to Heaven in Book 10:

> To him with swift ascent he up returnd,
> Into his blissful bosom reassum'd
> In glory as of old, to him appeas'd
> All, though all-knowing, what had past with Man
> Recounted, mixing intercession sweet.
>
> [10.224–28]

The interesting language that Milton chooses to describe this reunion well indicates the complexity of the idea of two-in-one. The Son is "reassum'd / In glory as of old," as though he had been gone for ages, although he has returned swiftly from a very brief visit to earth. Perhaps the language emphasizes the importance of what the Son has just done, the way in which it has not only decided the future of mankind, but anticipated it. Also, he tells God what God already knows, because without the Son (whom he cannot be without), God is not omniscient. In fact, when the Son walks in the garden, he is called God. But the distinctive characteristics of Father and Son are also emphasized in the contrast between the one who has to be appeased and the sweet intercessions of the appeaser. The reconciliation of opposites that goes on in this passage foreshadows, as does so much in the poem, the time when time will not exist, and God will be all in all.

God's consciousness at the beginning emerged from Chaos, the abyss, or coexisted with it, the first cave. With consciousness came recognition of division and death, time and mortality, and the creation of the second cave, that of Hell. But from the beginning there is also apprehension of fulfillment in eternity, an apprehension conveyed finally to Adam and Eve at the end of Book 12:

> He ended; and thus *Adam* last reply'd.
> How soon hath thy prediction, Seer blest,
> Measur'd this transient World, the Race of time,
> Till time stand fixt: beyond is all abyss,
> Eternitie, whose end no eye can reach.

> [12.552–56]

Thus are the limits described for everything that can happen in the epic. From the abyss, consciousness emerges, and beyond itself it looks toward the abyss at the end. Only the forecast of human history delivered by Michael could enable Adam to experience release from history in transcendent knowledge. Because God accepted his own involvement in history, Adam can also paradoxically find transcendence by accepting time. Finally, the pun on the word "eye" reminds us that it was Satan's egocentric, self-seeking nature that caused death, his refusal to accept his own immersion in a greater force. The abyss of eternity remains as inaccessible to the "I" as is the original abyss of Chaos.

Humanity exists between two kinds of nothingness, the primal cave and the final abyss. The effort to make a mark in the world is natural to fallen man. In "Lycidas" Milton calls it the last infirmity of noble mind. But it is a striving against redeemed nature, or even against the most honest self-consciousness, because it runs counter to the awareness of whatever loss of self eternity may represent. All epic poets have dealt with this problem, by at least acknowledging the significance of eternity, and by undercutting the epic hero's particular goals. But Milton tried to relieve the stress by bringing God and man closer together, and directly connecting eternity with time. The tension is thus turned into Christian paradox, and the way is prepared for a human being, even in a fallen world, to become one with God. The pattern for that achievement is set forth in *Paradise Regained*.

III

Paradise Regained

Perhaps the most significant event in *Paradise Lost* is the begetting of the Son, for it instigates every other action of the poem, both evil and good. It sets forth God's purpose as creator, and initiates our understanding of the necessary divisiveness of creation, of which even God may not have been fully aware. It also affirms God's commitment to creation, which remains steady even when he understands that the Son himself, his own creative power, must become subject to death. At the same time that it separates it unites: its expressed intention is to bring the order of angels nearer to God, and it will be so employed toward humankind as well. Yet to some extent, the first ten books of *Paradise Lost* remain abstract demonstrations for us, concentrated as they are on beginnings, and on worlds beyond the here and now. Although we are the result of it all, inherent in the lives of Adam and Eve, and in the creative characters of God and the Son, we do not directly see ourselves until the fall and the subsequent historical survey of Books 11 and 12.

I have shown that the uniqueness of these two books is in their placement at the end of the poem, and in the possibility offered to each historical person to transcend time, becoming heroic or demonic, and to accept or reject life and the concomitant fact of death. That is the same rubric that the Christian reader already has in the Bible. But *Paradise Regained* [1] both illustrates and explains the rubric, in singling out the story of one man, the Son of God, whose singular obedience to God provides a full description of the affirmation of life in the midst of death.

Appropriately the poem begins with another kind of revelation, a sign by God, to the world, of Jesus' Sonship. This revelation, like the begetting in *Paradise Lost*, sets off much of what follows, since it provides Satan's motivation; it is a provoking action as well as a reconciling one. It is impossible not to be aware of this fact in relation to the begetting. And, from the beginning, it is impossible not to think of this poem in relation to *Paradise Lost*. Despite the difficulties that readers have always had with its spare simplicity (which some think of as provoking harshness), it demands to be read, not just as a sequel to *Paradise Lost*, but as its fruition, completion, and mirror image. Edward Phillips said that *Paradise Regained* "doubtless was begun and finished and printed after the other [*Paradise Lost*] was publisht"; [2] it was licensed on July 2, 1670. In every possible way it grew out of the earlier poem.

Yet it is a whole poem in its own right, one that uses and depends upon the whole tradition behind it, including *Paradise Lost*. In fact, its opening line—"I who e're while the happy Garden sung"—suggests that, compared to this, *Paradise Lost* was a mere youthful pastoral,[3] and it is said that Milton very much disliked unfavorable comparisons of *Paradise Regained* with *Paradise Lost*. *Paradise Lost* is an epic about God, justifying God's ways. *Paradise Regained* is a description of a man's response to God's ways, taking upon himself and fully using the godhood inherent in his creation. One might say that it would have been irresponsible of Milton to stop at the end of *Paradise Lost*. Although the blueprint for fallen humanity is there in the last two books, it is esthetically difficult for readers to pay enough attention to it. Milton needed to make another poem to right the balance and return epic history to human nature.

It is true that Milton has now deprived himself of much of the epic machinery that he employed in *Paradise Lost*. Half of that was derided in Satan; the rest he thought appropriate to transcendence. The God who was out there, in Heaven and in Paradise, had to be accorded a sublimity not due to fallen human nature. At the same time Milton wanted to deride what he considered the fallen and distorted use of that kind of language to describe epic heroism. He succeeded in *Paradise Lost* in having things both ways. For *Paradise Regained* that was no longer possible.

It is tempting to apply to these two epics the Puritans' distinction between the Anglican wisdom of words, and their own Word of Wisdom, between the baroque high style and the Puritan Word of God indwelling in simple, direct expression.[4] The distinction is accurate if we recognize how fully Milton has adapted the two styles to his own particular needs, which required both appreciative and derogatory use of grandeur in *Paradise Lost*. The sense of transcendence, the correspondence between outer magnificence and inner light, the fitness of everything in its own place in relation to everything else—all these could appropriately be expressed in the older style. In *Paradise Regained* Milton needs to describe a world in which good is practically indistinguishable from evil (as explained in *Areopagitica*) and the power of insight is crucial. In order to provide that experience, he has to force the reader to look within. Instead of the sort of outer spaciousness we experience in *Paradise Lost,* therefore, the spaciousness is all to be found within the words and actions which readmit us to Paradise in the spaciousness of the soul. The style is pointed inward. Wordplay, mirroring, typology, and other such devices, already present in *Paradise Lost,* become much more important, though perhaps less immediately obvious.

The most important stylistic characteristic of *Paradise Lost* which *Paradise Regained* retains and intensifies is its power to gather into itself so much Judaeo-Christian history and literature. Because Milton's subject is the life of Jesus, which Christian exegetes for centuries had seen foreshadowed everywhere in the Old Testament and in profane history and literature, he has access to all that material almost without having to claim it explicitly. Because only an unusual reader would come to *Paradise Regained* without benefit of *Paradise Lost,* Milton can use mirroring on almost every page to increase the resonance of the later poem, assuring the fact of its epic stature in relation to *Paradise Lost* and its tradition. Further, the poem seems to reflect and complete all of Milton's other major poetical works, and of course many of the political tracts as well. Specifically, it illuminates and is nourished by the "Nativity Ode," because of its portrayal of the relationship between Jesus and the world; *Comus,* because of its temptation in the wilderness; *Paradise Lost,* which it directly follows; and *Samson Agonistes,* the temptation story with which it was first published. Because of all these circumstances, Milton did not need more than four short books for this poem. Despite its spareness, it is as intense and resonant as any of its predecessors in the epic line.

Paradise Lost is staged in the cosmos and its caves, *Paradise Regained* in the human cave alone. The poem is suffused with the language of doubt. Despite the clarity of the Son's credentials as discovered by himself, attested by John the Baptist, and affirmed by God, no one around him, with the possible exception of his mother, understands what they mean. The disciples, being as sure as Satan that the kingdom is to be a worldly one, are shaken by his disappearance; his mother is at least distressed, though accustomed to patience. Satan, who should be prepared to understand better than anyone else, is or makes himself ignorant of whether this is the Son of God he once knew, or some other. In varying degrees, these characters allow doubt to affect them, and doubt is the first temptation that Satan offers Jesus in the wilderness. It is the first condition of living in a fallen world, the direct result of the fall, that self-knowledge, or God-knowledge in its original simplicity, has been obscured.

This is the atmosphere in which Jesus is revealed. At once he is led into further caves, whose literal and metaphorical aspects are not entirely distinct:

> Mean while the Son of God, who yet some days
> Lodg'd in *Bethabara* where John baptiz'd,
> Musing and much revolving in his brest,
> How best the mighty work he might begin
> Of Saviour to mankind, and which way first
> Publish his God-like office now mature,
> One day forth walk'd alone, the Spirit leading;
> And his deep thoughts, the better to converse
> With solitude, till far from track of men,
> Thought following thought, and step by step led on,
> He entred now the bordering Desert wild,

And with dark shades and rocks environ'd round,
His holy Meditations thus persu'd.

[1.183–95]

In Book 2 we will be told explicitly that Jesus "into himself descended," but the process here is clear enough. He follows the lead of his own spirit without fear and without regard to the consequences:

The way he came not having mark'd, return
Was difficult, by human steps untrod. . . .

[1.297–98]

That difficult return *has* been marked in previous epics, but remains hard and unique, for every adventurer finds the cave the same and yet different from those of his ancestors. This landscape is highly symbolic, a pictorial confusion of material described as "a pathless Desert, dusk with horrid shades," containing shady vales, caves, ancient trees, wild beasts, a woody maze, double-shading night. The word "shade" in more than one sense is frequently used. It is a place both empty of any apparent resources and full of danger. It is the salt desert and waste wilderness that used to be Eden, the wood in which Adam and Eve hid themselves after the fall, the cave and wood of the unconscious as portrayed in so many previous epics, and the landscape of Jesus' own mind.

There is no question, then, that he is in a cave, and that he is there because as a human being he, like Odysseus, has to explore the dark places of the mind in order to know himself. That the wild beasts grow tame at his approach does not entirely obviate the problem. That incident at once reminds us of a wide range of previous epic moments —Una's lion in the *Faerie Queene*, Dante's beasts in the

Inferno (from which he is saved by Beatrice), the restoration of the landscape of Heaven in *Paradise Lost* at the approach of the Son. Una also calls to mind the Lady of Comus who, like Una, cannot be harmed in the wilderness because of the integrity of her virtue. Shining the light of consciousness or virtue into the darkness does alleviate its terrors. But in none of these instances is the darkness vanquished. Thus it is worthwhile to accept all these parallels with a kind of literal-mindedness that allows us to see Jesus as a human being involved in an experience familiar to epic and other literary (and nonliterary) characters, both male and female. Nothing that he does in *Paradise Regained* is out of human reach.

In this poem the sense of transcendence so present in *Paradise Lost* is missing until the end of the fourth book. That abstract force for life which is God, whose presence especially informs the descriptions of Heaven and Eden, is gone. At the beginning of the poem we are treated to a brief appearance of the God of *Paradise Lost*, Book 3, who comes in to give the Son his credentials. At this time he names Jesus both man and Son of God, says that the experience in the wilderness is to be a chance for him to make use of his own nature, and calls him to the attention of the world, especially Satan. The function he fulfills is almost entirely mechanical; as in the earlier poem, only more so, he must be regarded as an extremely limited aspect of the whole process and being that is God.

It is more important, and more difficult, to understand who Jesus is. Satan spends the whole poem trying to figure that out. He is emphatically introduced as a man, and it has to be our first assumption that he really is one. He is not a mouthpiece for God or a spirit in human dress. He is altogether and unequivocally human. But he is also intended to make clear to anyone willing to pay attention that, at least from this time forward, all people have the power of divinity within, if they can come to terms with the fact of death. In the light of epic tradition, and in *Paradise Regained,* this is a crucially important paradox, and one which will require further clarification during the whole course of this essay.

A continuing problem in classical epic was the "godlike" hero who, if he became one of the immortals, would cease to be godlike in any sense that human beings aspire to, since because the Olympian gods are free of death they cannot engage in heroic struggle. But for Milton's Jesus the central issue of human struggle is to recognize that the power death has in the world is owing to fallen humanity's willingness to submit to its machinery while rejecting its existence—that is, to engage in futile and death-dealing "epic" struggles for power and glory. The Son's is a struggle simply for the affirmation of life, the winning of which is union with the divine. In other words, in *Paradise Lost* we see God taking on mortality, and in *Paradise Regained* we see mortality claiming for all time that presence of God within.

This interchange does not entirely solve the artistic dilemma, but at least it is rationalized in Milton's esthetics, as in his theology. The art he intended to create when England became Utopia would have been a unique art of praise, which only redeemed ears were capable of enjoying. In that more distant time when "God shall be all in all," so that creator and created are one, the question of art is subsumed into a larger question—the whole character of creation at the end of time—which life in process can never

answer. What makes Milton's universe appear more satisfying than that of the classical gods and heroes is that
everything, including God, is in process, so that the imagined splendor at the end is never thought of as static, and
is a mystery as yet unknown, foreshadowed only in transcendent moments in which time itself is abolished.

The confronting of this problem in classical epic seems
to lead to the solution of another problem, that of the discrepancy between the hero's apparent and real goals. As a
subversive form, the epic calls in question the goals of the
hero's community or culture. Yet it was impossible for
Achilles or Aeneas to become realized without fighting the
Trojan war or striving to found the Roman Empire. The
purpose of Jesus' struggle is to avoid founding the empire
or doing any of the other things to which epic heroes have
been forced to commit their lives. Where each of those
"later" heroes is responsible for one all-important task,
Jesus is to reject all such tasks, regarding them as the de-
lusive activities of fallen men. His work is to demonstrate
the possibility of "repairing the ruins of our first parents
by regaining to know God aright." That has always been
the purpose of epic, achieved through the education of hero
and reader, while the hero goes on about his active business
in the world. Now all the discrepancies are resolved, as
the regaining of Paradise becomes the explicit goal, a subversive effort undertaken against the worldly kingdom of
Satan.

The poem is short because it assumes that we have read
Paradise Lost, and can recognize the intentional trans-
formations and contrasts. It can also be short because it is
completely folded in upon itself; everything that is objectified expansively in *Paradise Lost* is here subjective

and compressed. Jesus does not have to do something in the course of which he enters into some caves. Everything that he has to do is acknowledged to be within. He is the first epic hero of whom we are explicitly told that he descended into himself.

Jesus' self-consciousness, at the beginning of the poem, is extreme. In other epics, entering *in medias res,* we have learned earlier episodes from the poet or from the character talking to someone else. Jesus is alone when we first meet him and, engrossed in himself, considers his past life in some detail. His mind seems especially to be struggling to fit external with internal reality, and to interpret correctly his messianic calling:

> O what a multitude of thoughts at once
> Awakn'd in me swarm, while I consider
> What from within I feel my self, and hear
> What from without comes often to my ears,
> Ill sorting with my present state compar'd.
>
> [1.196–200]

He has had no dealings, save at baptism, with an exterior manifestation of God. He has no remembrance of a former heavenly state, and no knowledge of his future except what he has learned from his own thoughts, his mother, and study of Scripture. What his mother told him about his birth and the assumptions of others about his mission are sufficiently intimidating, and he has been drawn to the idea of physical conquest, although he prefers to try first to free people without violence. But although beseiged by his own hopes and those of others, the only certainties he has are that he is the Messiah promised in Scripture, and that he is going to have to die in order to attain the kingdom and work redemption. This apparent paradox he has already accepted, and, despite the burden of his tumultuous thoughts, he has also accepted the idea that he must live in patient ignorance.

Where Adam and Eve ended by taking on mortality and then hearing of their own future and mankind's, Christ begins, in the more usual way of epic heroes, by hearing and reading about himself and his descent. He is no different from other heroes in his knowledge of semidivine birth, no different in being somehow set apart. However, his recognition of his mortality is more immediate than usual, as is the linking of his death to the success of his quest. These things, and no others, at the outset distinguish Jesus as a character from other epic heroes, and they are not matters which could in any way invalidate his heroic stature. The knowledge of mortality is, after all, universally available. What Jesus does not yet know is that his work is to destroy death itself by unmasking its pretenses. That work is humanly available, but a great deal more difficult, as Milton reasonably argues, than the usual heroic quest.

Readers trained to a different kind of epic and a different conception of Christianity have had trouble with *Paradise Regained* on this score. If in *Paradise Lost* Satan is too compelling a figure, here a major complaint is that he is too weak. If Jesus is God, then of course he is not tempted, the duel is without real conflict, and the story becomes esthetically invalid. To some extent, I think we have already gotten beyond this dilemma. Jesus' understanding of himself is that he is Messiah, which is not the same thing as God. God is more involved in human pain and limitation than the traditional Christian Deity, in any case, and so no matter what the extent of Jesus' understanding of himself, he can never wholly transcend humanity.

Recognition of the extent of Satan's significance has with good reason been inadequate. Because of the spare infoldedness of the poem, he combines within himself functions much more widely distributed in previous epics. Of course he has long been seen as both an objective force and an aspect of Jesus' own consciousness, just as in *Paradise Lost* Hell is both an external place and a state of mind. Satan is the dark side of human nature, Jesus' shadow, a part of himself that Jesus is engaged in cutting free. He is also, in himself, a full demonstration of everything that Milton had by 1670 concluded about the evils of the self-assertive individual ego, and of external things. Thus he serves as Jesus' unconscious, tempter, twin, and foil; as his antagonist; and as link with and representative of that work which it is Jesus' heroic task to perform.

Much of this is obvious, and it is only the last point which requires elaboration now. The course of human consciousness as charted in classical epic has shown us the struggle of the hero to lift himself into awareness, to individuate himself from the unconscious and become whole. Yet the process of individuation is a separating and alienating one, which denies the kind of integrity with all things that originally existed. By a wide range of devices, consciousness is used to transcend itself and to bring the mature person back to wholeness. Satan is one of the first modern examples of a totally alienated being, cut off by his own actions from any possibility of relationship or wholeness or redemption. Milton saw the connection between individualism, technology, and alienation, and demonstrated it in many ways, in both *Paradise Lost* and *Paradise Regained*, but most particularly in this diminished figure.

Satan's original rebellion against God seemed much like any heroic struggle for consciousness, except that it was done in reverse. He was at the outset in the position of most epic heroes when they are at the end of quest; in that prelapsarian cosmos, he had integrity with the whole of life, which was God. Falling backward, the only place he could move, the only direction different from God's direction, was death, which he chose because it was the only alternative to God and not because it was death. Faced with his own work, as when he meets Death at the gate of Hell, he is simultaneously moved to disown and to embrace it. His situation is impossible. He can seem to have what he wants only by embodying contradiction, choosing to become death without letting himself know what he has done.

At the same time he lets death loose upon the universe, Milton is well aware of the applicability to postlapsarian life of the description of worldly power in the Book of Revelation. When Death and Sin take over and Satan becomes god of the earth, everything in it becomes an instrument of death in its material form. This is the meaning of the two cities of Revelation, of Babylon and Jerusalem. Babylon is this world under Satan. Jerusalem is this world under God. They exist simultaneously, superimposed upon each other. Babylon is the only one that Satan can recognize, and it is synonymous with death.

The dilemma, in different form, is familiar to epic poetry, which had always concerned itself with the difference between appearance and reality. Ariosto's rejection of external things is in its way as categorical as Milton's, although his is finally a senseless universe, and Milton's is not. In the *Orlando Furioso* good and evil exist side by side, in similar and indistinguishable forms, and it is impossible to tell which is which, or even to know that a particular thing, once identified, will maintain its identity. There is no question of searching below or beyond appearances to get to the truth. Ariosto certainly has no Christian solution to this problem, since for him Christianity is as pointless as everything else. To deal with the world is to learn that you cannot deal with it. His art gives him a kind of magicianship that enables him to see life as funny; symbols like Angelica's magic ring suggest the possibility of gaining enough transcendence over material things to become indifferent to them.

To us, one of the most attractive features of Ariosto's poem is his recognition of our unending vulnerability. And with the perversity of fallen nature, we are chilled by Milton's assumption that one can be, not invulnerable perhaps, but unwounded. Such a condition seems to us inhuman, as well as unreachable and meaningless. Milton would agree with Ariosto about what the world looks like. But for him it looks like that because it is controlled by death, and death can be overcome. Jesus regains Paradise by learning indifference to the works of death, and by seeing death as the barrier thrown up by Satan between human nature and life, which is also eternity. To do so, he must relinquish his own ego. The central issue of his heroic task thus comes to be identical with the rewards of previous heroes. The epic embrace that signals what momentary transcendence of self-consciousness they can achieve is transformed here into his direct confrontation and transcendence of his own consciousness. At the very beginning of the poem, at the very moment that we find in Jesus as self-conscious a hero as any epic has portrayed, he relinquishes personal control over his own destiny. He has been led into the desert by the promptings of his spirit, not his will, and he believes that "what concerns my knowledge God reveals."

When Satan first appears, Milton bridges the gap between *Paradise Lost* and *Paradise Regained* with a pun on the name of Eve:

> But now an aged man, in Rural weeds,
> Following, as seem'd, the quest of some stray Ewe,
> Or wither'd sticks to gather; which might serve
> Against a Winters day when winds blow keen,
> To warm him wet return'd from field at Eve,
> He saw approach, who first with curious eye
> Perus'd him, then with words thus utt'red spake.
>
> [1.314–20]

Not only does the linkage through Eve establish Satan's role as tempter backward and forward; it also shows at once that evil has recoiled upon itself. Although Satan chose his own disguise, it is particularly emblematic of a fallen world, whose conditions are age, wandering, withering, winter, cold, and wet. The phrase "curious eye," which significantly repeats the "eye-I" pun at the end of *Paradise Lost*, establishes a central motif of all the temptations, and another linkage with *Paradise Lost*, as well as with earlier epics, since it signals the familiar theme of curiosity over against wisdom, external learning versus self-knowledge. Finally, Satan comes on in the guise of a shepherd, attempting, as he will do throughout, to obliterate superficially the distinction between himself and Jesus.

Like all Milton's tempters, Satan encourages Jesus to become what he already is or will be. He consistently ma-

terializes, or literalizes, biblical prophecy, unable to per-
ceive the spiritual dimension which alone applies to the life
of Jesus. This is the scientizing according to which Satan
becomes a modern jack-of-all-trades and master of none,
a knowledge-and-real-estate broker who takes delight in
such gadgets as the "airy microscope" by which he enables
Jesus to view all the kingdoms of the world. Whether or
not this is Mount Niphates, from which Michael gave
Adam visionary wisdom, the difference in method and intention is purposeful. The most direct of all these temptations, in respect to their attempt to substitute curiosity for
self-knowledge, is Athens, where philosophers sit, like the
devils in *Paradise Lost,* discoursing of "fate, and chance,
and change in human life" (4.265). Milton's attitude toward learning is the same as it was when in 1645 he pre-
scribed a curriculum designed to repair the ruins of our
first parents. Knowledge not directed toward that end is
idle; the learning of Greece, which Jesus already has, is
only useful in the light of the Gospel. That is, it is only
useful with reference to Jesus' life, and must go to school
to him, not he to it. The temptation parallels Adam's unnecessary desire to know astronomy. The heavens may be
studied to God's glory, but at this particular time his curiosity simply leads Adam away from himself and the field
where his attention needs to be focused.

In that simpler world it was easy enough for Adam to
see that astronomy was not for him, but a way of describing the fall is in terms of the multiple choices and accompanying anxieties that are the fate of modern man. Almost
everything that Adam wanted to do was right; decision
was scarcely a part of his life. With the confusion of good

and evil, even innocent decisions come to rule every minute of the day, preventing clear understandings. Satan is
accustomed to that kind of environment and is himself
paralyzed by it, as shown by his inability to know who the
Son of God is or how to confront him. The problems that
he brings to Jesus are almost all complex and worldly: is
it all right to eat shellfish; can a man accept food from his
enemy; which kingdom makes the best ally; when is the
right time for action; what sort of bibliography is needed
to impress the opposition? Jesus' recognition that all these
questions are irrelevant is the only means to relieve such
paralysis and obtain again the freedom of the garden.

In these scenes, Jesus rejects the role of the epic hero
who pursues his quest as a flawed man in a flawed world.
And Milton, like Dante, rejects the compromise inherent
in a tradition that assumes a man must work out his fate
within the available culture. If all worldly acts are tainted,
are in fact no more real actions than the repeated chewing
of the ashy fruit in Hell, that is because understanding of
real action is absent, and another kind of vision is required.
It is necessary for the hero to be a prophet. I have already
mentioned the extensive use of language having to do with
ignorance and doubt in this poem. It combines with the
pressure Satan exerts upon Jesus to choose among multiple
unsatisfactory alternatives, and with the curiosity motif
that is attached to Satan himself. The more one tries to
know in a worldly sense, the less one knows. If on one
level Satan seems jaded and worldly-wise, in a more fundamental way he is absolutely ignorant, described as being
in a perpetual state of amazement. That is the condition of
the creature who informs the oracles, providing the most

accepted source of information to the world, which is pervaded with rumors and lies.

Opposing all this is Jesus' initial recognition of Satan: "I discern thee other than thou seem'st" (1.348). The key word is repeated at the end of the storm temptation: "desist, thou art discerned" (4.497). It is an important word in biblical history. Discernment is one of the charismatic gifts described by St. Paul as belonging to the primitive church (1 Cor. 12.10), and it refers to the power of insight, especially at crucial times of spiritual decision. It requires extensive self-knowledge; in fact the literature concerning it occasionally employs the same language for the unconscious that is customary in the epic. Thus, Cassian, arguing the importance of spiritual guidance preparatory to distinguishing the divine from the diabolical within: "In virtue of this confession the loathsome serpent is brought to light from out of the dark, subterranean cavern." [5] Jesus' power to maintain and fulfill his integrity against Satan's assaults comes in part from his use of discernment, which is our key to the real work that he is doing in the poem. The literature shows the centrality of the temptation in the wilderness in Christ's life. He is the only person who ever encounters Satan undisguised, clearly recognizing the loathsome serpent in himself and unmasking his pretences. "His whole work on earth will be to lead men to recognize. . . . the ways of the Spirit," [6] that is, to do what he himself has done. After self-knowledge, the unmasking of external things becomes easier.

Satan also uses the term "discernment"—he apes everything that Jesus does—but, by applying it to a secondary issue, he immediately obfuscates and diminishes any power it could have had to begin with in his mind:

A Kingdom they [the stars] portend thee, but what Kingdom,
Real or Allegoric I discern not. . . .

[4.389–90]

For Jesus, all the kingdom and glory of the world is discerned as Babylon, and thereby discredited, made micro-
scopic beside his true inheritance.

Discernment can only be practiced in abnegation of one's
own ego; otherwise it would lead to self-deception. Thus
the work of discernment combines with the Son's openness
to spiritual leading. These activities appear passive from a
worldly point of view. However, the language of the
poem directs us to reconstitute our view of what activity is.
Both the poet and God describe the action of the poem in
military language, and Mary fosters Jesus' self-knowledge
in words reminiscent of the poet-hero of *Paradise Lost:*

High are thy thoughts
O Son, but nourish them and let them soar
To what highth sacred vertue and true worth
Can raise them, though above example high;
By matchless Deeds express thy matchless Sire.

[1.229–33]

As she intuitively begins to blur the distinction between
thought and action, she recalls for us the Son of *Paradise
Lost* by her use of the word "express" (1.234). The regaining of Paradise is to be achieved through rejection of
superficial action and recovery of the capacity to be at one
with God.

I have discussed the necessity for earlier epic heroes to
maintain a stern self-discipline, the control that tunes them
consistently to a more expansive consciousness and self-
consciousness than are possessed by other men. Both the

journey into the psyche and the journey through the world (as they are different and as they are one) require such vigilance. And sometimes that self-discipline breaks down toward the end when it seems most needed, but perhaps at the time when the hero can best afford to lose control. Partly because his consciousness is so completely capable of rejecting Satan and his works, and because his recognition of them is so complete, Jesus, like Dante, is not subject to that kind of relapse. Rather, the violence is all expressed by Satan, whose self-control is undependable from the beginning. As always, he apes the heroic stance, losing control of himself more and more disastrously as the poem nears its end. Redemption requires the casting out of one's own devils. In Satan Jesus confronts all that is barbarous and degraded in human nature—all the wild men, devils, pagans of the tradition—and renders it impotent merely by recognizing it for what it is.

Almost every comparison of *Paradise Regained* with its predecessors reveals another way in which Satan has been made the machinery with which to fold in an epic device. The temptations which the hero encounters on his journey are a reason for self-control, and one important kind of temptation is toward loss of consciousness, especially in false gardens, in madness, or in suicide. Satan provides Jesus the opportunity for all three of these, in the banquet, the storm, and the pinnacle.

The banquet, which is neither in the Bible nor in tradition, has sometimes been thought oddly anticlimactic, another eating temptation after the much more compelling suggestion to turn stones into bread. And in a way it is that: Satan has a talent for anticlimax that tinges the whole poem with comedy. But it is more important to see the epi-

sode as garden than as banquet, for, just as Eden foreshadows in its perfection all possible and lesser future gardens,
this scene recalls and finally dismisses them.

Satan has constructed a "pleasant grove," artfully
equipped with chanting birds, bowers, walks, and varying
shade. The table stands "in ample space under the broadest
shade" (2.339), and there is much coming and going of
youths and maidens, besides the sound of music, and winds
carrying sweet odors. So it is in itself a spacious place, and
it seems even more so because of the allusions to Eden, to
Armida's garden, and the world of chivalric romance:

> Alas how simple, to these Cates compar'd,
> Was that crude Apple that diverted *Eve!*
>
> [2.349–50]

The virtuosity of the production is just another illustration
of the kind of power Satan has over the world. Technology can make a garden bloom in the desert, art can bemuse
with richly layered associations, and casuistry can devise
choices with no right answer. If Jesus refuses to eat shellfish, he is acceding to the old law, and if he agrees, he ac-
cedes to Satan.

Jesus' dreams of eating, preceding this scene, parallel
the dream given Eve before the fall, and the religious associations with prophets fed in the wilderness are meant to
allow him to follow the typological blueprints. Even more
important, perhaps, the idea that this is a Communion table
responds to Jesus' hunger, which he has just mentioned, to
do his father's will. The false gardens of previous epics
accommodate the heroes' desire both to forget themselves
and to save their lives. Satan knows enough not to make
this one harbor the annihilating witch-woman. Instead,

the implied Communion suggests both self-preservation (which Satan again urges upon Jesus) and loss of self in God. But Jesus would have to play God self-consciously in yielding to temptation, and the annihilator would be Satan.

Having lost this engagement, Satan allows the machinery to clank as the props are removed. It was the artful perspectives of the scene that enchanted, the sense of cool spaciousness in the desert; the speed with which the illusion is destroyed proves it to be more like a mirage. The scene is intended to remind us that, blooming or not, the desert remains desert, and Paradise cannot be artificially regained.

The temptation to madness is implicit in Jesus' situation,[7] in the discrepancy that he perceives between his thoughts and his condition. Because he sees the world accurately, as a desert, he is able to withstand temptation to worldly prizes. Yet his inner knowledge that he is to be a king conflicts with his apparent state of destitution, and with everyone else's ideas of what a king should be. Madness is a particular threat in solitude, as the Desert Fathers knew: the more risks one takes to get close to God, the greater the chance of failure. Milton does not use this information directly in the poem, but he does not need to; it is an obvious aspect of his conflict with the Satan in himself.

This temptation reaches its climax in the storm scene. Having used up all his bait, Satan in effect accuses Jesus of being out of his mind:

> Since neither wealth, nor honour, arms nor arts,
> Kingdom nor Empire pleases thee, nor aught
> By me propos'd in life contemplative,

Or active, tended on by glory, or fame,
What dost thou in this World? the Wilderness
For thee is fittest place. . . .

[4.368–73]

He continues to argue that Jesus has lost the chance to be
Messiah, that the stars promise for him suffering and
death, and, if a kingdom, one as much without beginning
as without end. Now Jesus is enveloped in darkness, and
beset with ugly dreams, ghosts, and furies, as well as a violent storm. It is a temptation to terror combined with further effort to undermine his self-confidence, for he is meant
to believe that the storm was aimed at him by God because
of his obstinacy. The unusual word "unappall'd," used to
describe Jesus' reaction to all this, emphasizes the uniqueness of his resistance. The word "appalled" is generally
attached to a situation which is appalling, in which it would
be impossible to remain calm, as he does. Satan had not
hoped to drive him out of his mind in the usual sense, for
in that sense he is already crazy. Rather, he wanted to
make him responsive to worldly lures (a fool before God)
by scaring him out of his crazy ideas. It is when Satan
returns in the morning that Jesus says to him, "desist,
thou art discern'd" (4.497).

There is no temptation that does not urge spiritual suicide upon its victims. Even the paradise temptation is to
suicide, for submitting to any such lure causes a person to
diminish himself to a greater or lesser degree. The scene
on the pinnacle simply carries that notion to its fullest
stretch, tempting to both spiritual and physical death. It
has also been called an attempted murder, and there is no
contradiction in that description; the words simply imply a

difference in the amount of externality with which Satan is viewed.

Satan is in a suicidal mood. During most of the proceedings, it has been clear that he is the edgy, desperate one; Jesus repeatedly observes that, and Satan admits it himself. Like most people, he would be everything or nothing:

> For where no hope is left, is left no fear;
> If there be worse, the expectation more
> Of worse torments me then the feeling can.
> I would be at the worst; worst is my Port,
> My harbour and my ultimate repose,
> The end I would attain, my final good.
>
> [3.206–11]

He is not resigned to that. Even in the course of the same speech, he continues strongly to urge glory upon Jesus, and to suggest the possibility that Jesus may befriend him when he comes into his kingdom. But he is very obviously a lost soul of the kind seen in Dante's *Inferno*, creatures who keep on with the motions of living, knowing and not knowing where they really are.

Yet although the odds seem so clearly divided between the suicidal Satan and the assured Jesus, the poem contains real struggle, unconventionally expressed. From Jesus' side, to discern Satan accurately requires a gathered act of concentration that does not permit the appearance of ordinary conflict. In order to succeed, he has to free himself of the kind of tension so evident in Satan and in most epic endeavor. He is not screwing himself up to do anything. He cannot try to kill Satan, as Aeneas can kill Turnus or as the Puritans killed Charles I. All the tension that would have to be expressed in some kind of violence must be abandoned to Satan himself.

Jesus knows that Satan has permission to try him, because that is the condition of life under the fall. He can do nothing to undo that permission except to recognize it for what it is. A violent or anxious response would implicate him and strengthen Satan. Even at the end, when "Satan smitten with amazement fell," he is not permanently gone. The fall will occur again, and Satan will always be smitten with amazement, just as he was in *Paradise Lost*. As the work of Jesus is to discern, the nonwork of Satan is to act in utter ignorance.

Jesus' descent into himself reveals this dark aspect of human nature for what it is, and his ability to face and acknowledge it totally, without fear, and without effort to destroy it, is what enables his self-mastery. The temptation to worship Satan, which appears so gratuitous, is psychologically valid in the sequence. Like others, it has its comic aspect, being an anticlimactic follow-up to the offer of all the kingdoms of the world. But in the preceding speech, Jesus has himself raised a direct challenge:

> I shall, thou say'st, expel
> A brutish monster: what if I withal
> Expel a Devil who first made him such?
> [4.127–29]

During the whole sequence, Satan's effort has been to distract Jesus from the relationship between them, and to make him consider his role in relation to the world. And never more so than in the temptation to take over the world, in which Satan offers the prospect of freeing all men from slavery. Jesus' response to this is Milton's, that men are responsible for their own enslavement, and there is no external redemption. Obviously, then, the implicit danger in this temptation has to be confronted: gain the world and lose your own soul. That is why Satan proposes this explicitly now.

The more nearly spiritual a temptation, the more real it is to a spiritual person, as is apparent in the whole history of this kind of literature—saints' lives, for instance. As long as the saint is tempted with material goods, there is no engagement of forces. To say "fall down and worship me" or "cast yourself down from the pinnacle" is much more compelling, just because it is in the same realm in which the saint lives. Here it is the all-out, last-gasp attempt of the exhausted shadow to compel. It only takes a minute to fall, not a gradual surrender to the almost imperceptible entrapments of the world. A relaxation of the tense mind, unwilled. That is why Jesus' disciplined lack of tension is so important. Either to try to kill Satan (excessive violence) or to give in to weariness and pride would be the obvious "heroic" response.

Throughout the poem Satan continues to imagine that he can identify and defeat Jesus with the same weapons that Milton's tempters have always used: in Eden, Eve is offered the opportunity to be more godlike than she already is, and thereby loses the majesty she possesses. Like Eve, Jesus needs no more status than he already has; unlike her, he is aware of that. He defeats Satan by asserting the power of humanity, which Satan has seen exercised in history only rarely, and never in such perfection. The title "Son of God," to which Satan repeatedly tempts Jesus to doubt his right, is a human one, belonging to all. At the climax of the poem, when Satan brings Jesus to the pinnacle of the temple, that doubt is expressed for the last time:

Now shew thy Progeny; if not to stand,
Cast thy self down; safely if Son of God:
For it is written, He will give command
Concerning thee to his Angels, in thir hands
They shall up lift thee, lest at any time
Thou chance to dash thy foot against a stone.

[4.554–59]

The passage is directly biblical, and entirely suited to its Miltonic context. The promise given in the Ninety-first Psalm has no more particular relevance to Jesus than to anyone else, and since it has been given it does not need to be invoked.

The reply, "Tempt not the Lord thy God," has in the Old Testament been a warning not to test God by asking for help, and that is an adequate meaning for it to have here too. The sentence is capable of implying Jesus' own assumption of godhood, but I think it contains that possibility simply in order not to exclude it—that is, in order to make the response as ambiguous as possible. Its specific explicit meaning is just that Jesus is not going to test God. At this moment he also demonstrates in his body his full understanding of his own nature.

Milton buttresses the moment of the Son's standing on the pinnacle with allusions to the conquest of Antaeus by Hercules, and Oedipus' solving of the riddle of the Sphinx. The first action is traditionally allegorized as victory of spirit over flesh. Because it is joined with the riddle whose solution is a definition of man, it would seem that Jesus is here defining true manhood by what he says and does. The victory of spirit over flesh is the victory over the death-dealing "external things" with which human beings living in history are ignorantly burdened. If he has here rejected suicide, he has prevented a repetition of the first human act of violence. He has restored human nature to itself by fully realizing the possibilities of human nature. Significantly, one of the external things of which he has not availed himself is God.

He is impervious to fear because he has transcended his own ego. From the beginning, he chooses not to worry about either his immediate or his long-range future. He is not concerned by the prophecy that he will gain his kingdom through suffering and death, or by the thunderstorm or the unstable footing on the pinnacle of the temple. At the beginning of *Paradise Lost*, Milton invoked, as his muse, the "Spirit, that dost prefer / Before all Temples th'upright heart and pure," for temples too are external things. It is appropriate for more than one reason that at the end of *Paradise Regained* the temple itself becomes a snare: "to stand upright," says Satan scornfully, "will ask thee skill." But Jesus has not been made dizzy by the prospect of the whole world spread out below him, and he is not made dizzy either by fear for his life. He is able to stand as a human being, resisting the downward pull of fallen humanity, because he is not burdened by egocentricity. Satan is that burden, and he falls away.

I have shown that Jesus' initial and primary weapon against Satan is discernment, the capacity given Christians to combat the effects of the fall. Those effects are described in this poem as clearly as in any other epic to be simply the indistinguishability of good from evil in the fallen mind, and the fact of self-consciousness itself, which is both curse and saving instrument. At the beginning of the poem, Jesus' self-consciousness has been fed in the same way as that of others. His own mind pulled him into awareness;

his mother told him his story; and he found his own history in the Bible. He is extremely self-analytical. Even when he is being led into the wilderness by the Spirit, he has to say to himself that the impulse is all right and that he need not know where it will take him.

Satan, in his many uses, provides the pairings that make self-consciousness so necessary and the world so hard to read in other epics. Throughout the poem the parallels between Satan and Jesus are stressed. Jesus is the Morning Star; Satan, Sun of the Morning, will fall from Heaven like a star. Satan tells us that he, like Jesus, is Son of God. Satan is god of this world, and believes that Jesus comes to inherit the same kingdom. In the sense in which he and his Father are one, Jesus is God in fact. Everything Jesus does or is meant to do, Satan does profanely. He descends from heaven, creates religions, speaks as an oracle, establishes kingdoms, and even carries out God's will, though not by his own choice. He is ignorantly worshiped by men. His city, Babylon, is juxtaposed in the world with Jesus' Jerusalem. He has been "emptied" (1.414), a word commonly used to describe Jesus at the Incarnation.

Both art and mirroring are involved in typological readings of the Bible, done by both Satan and Jesus. Satan's intention is always profane, materialistic, and goal-centered. Jesus reads to discover who he is, Satan to learn what to do. Satan repeatedly uses art in the poem in order to deceive: his artful paradise, his various disguises, the oratorical strategies of his speeches are all intended to prevent knowledge and cause sin.

We have seen throughout the history of the epic that self-knowledge cannot exist without relationship, which cannot exist without separation. All epic heroes learn to fulfill themselves through relationships, especially with women (mothers, lovers, witch-women), guest-friends, comrades, and fathers. At the same time they are often solitary and even unlikable because their energies are engaged on a level of consciousness unavailable to others. Jesus is the most solitary figure in all this long tradition; he speaks to no one but Satan, who may not even count as another person. But we have already seen that engagement in worldly activity, by which previous heroes have learned themselves, is now to be scorned, and Jesus is set off from his disciples for that very reason: he knows that his work is in the desert. He is not for that reason lacking in significant relationships, and the traditional figures of woman and father are central.

In Book 2, when Belial suggests temptation by women, both he and Satan speak at some length in what appears to be a gratuitous antifeminist digression. Women are beautiful, wanton lures, "more like to Goddesses / Than Mortal Creatures," "terrible to approach." The idea of the terrible enchantress-mother is very nakedly expressed, yet Satan, ignorant of Jesus as he elsewhere claims to be, and is, argues that "Beauty stands / In the admiration only of weak minds"; there is no woman, "though of this Age the wonder and the fame, / On whom his leisure will vouchsafe an eye / Of fond desire" (2.220–21, 209–11). The claim that only Belial's depraved sensuality could conceive of this temptation explains without justifying its elaboration. What may really justify it is that the episode gets rid of this traditional and significant use of woman as temptress in the epic, and calls attention to an important aspect of Jesus' uniqueness. It is not only that he is not weak-minded. There is no polarizing of male and female in his conscious-

ness, and the symbol of that is the continuity of his mind
with that of his mother. Early in Books 1 and 2, lengthy
parts of his destiny and biography are rehearsed in her
words; she says,

> My heart hath been a store-house long of things
> And sayings laid up, portending strange events.
>
> [2.103–4]

She has the usual role of one kind of strong female character, that of Penelope and Beatrice, who nourish and direct
the hero. Further, the storehouse of her mind has been
poured into his; he shaped himself partly upon her teaching. Unlike some other great mothers of epic, she has
never been coercive: she enables him to find himself, learns
that he cannot be lost, waits with patience for events
neither he nor she can fully understand. The emphasis on
his biography since childhood, on the many years of their
association, is unusual in epic; he has had no need to leave
her because their minds are trained to dwell both in and
outside of time. He has gone and will go much further
than her understanding, but never beyond her witness, and
as the story begins with the Incarnation, Jesus returns to
her house at the end of this poem.

Although solitary, he is never alone. His capacity for
union defines him; that is what he is here for. From the
beginning of the poem, Milton has him using Dantean
identification-language, as in his remembrance of the baptism. First John proclaims him the Messiah; then the Father asserts his Sonship:

> . . . but he
> Strait knew me, and with loudest voice proclaim'd
> Me him (for it was shew'n him so from Heaven)

Me him whose Harbinger he was; and first
Refus'd on me his Baptism to confer,
As much his greater. . . .
And last the sum of all, my Father's voice,
Audibly heard from Heav'n, pronounc'd me his,
Me his beloved Son, in whom alone
He was well pleas'd. . . .

[1.274–86]

The baptism episode corresponds to the epic convention of guest-friendship. The juxtaposed pronouns initially both identify Jesus with John (as in biblical typology) and emphasize Jesus' own identity; the two points are interdependent. John can recognize Jesus because the Son is John's fulfillment, and Jesus needs John's acknowledgment in order to become fulfilled. Then a similar juxtaposition occurs in the Father's language, except that now Jesus is not "him" but "his," identified as himself because he is his Father's Son. He is one with God, but not equal to God.

There has been much controversy among critics as to the extent of the Son's knowledge of himself in this poem, and also, for that matter, as to what his self really is. The fact that he is both human and divine does not make him different from other epic heroes. His life is intended as a pattern for everyone; he closes the gap between the epic hero and the common man, as well as between the hero and God. Knowing at the beginning of the poem that he is Messiah, he is in the wilderness to discover what that means. That is his epic task, for as he becomes revealed to himself, self-realization becomes available to mankind:

A fairer Paradise is founded now
For *Adam* and his chosen Sons. . . .

[4.613–14]

Although Jesus is the most explicitly self-conscious figure in the tradition, he is the least self-centered and the
least separated from all that surrounds him. The woman
closest to him is his mother; she has nourished both his
body and his consciousness with her own. Since he is the
fulfillment of which John the Baptist is the type, these two
men are in that sense to be seen as one person. As second
Adam, Jesus is all human beings, and as redeemer he is of
God. Near the beginning of the poem, Satan in his invinci-
ble ignorance accurately describes the Son:

> Who this is we must learn, for man he seems
> In all his lineaments, though in his face
> The glimpses of his Fathers glory shine.
>
> [1.91–93]

It is the same way in which the Son in *Paradise Lost* is
characteristically described. In humanity, God's glory is a
transforming presence, which rightly seems to Satan paradoxical, although he himself has no capacity for paradox.
In Jesus, self-consciousness is turned into God-consciousness; that is his epic achievement.

As all readers have recognized, it is difficult to use accurate language with regard to what occurs in Jesus' mind
in this poem. This is not a bildungsroman; there is no
character development, yet he is in the wilderness for a
reason. As so often happens, one of the easiest literary
analogies is with Homer, whose characters are also lacking in egocentricity. Jesus' temptations are like the experiences of Odysseus. They try, and manifest his spirit. But
where Odysseus comes at the beginning of a tradition that
is to separate men from their Calypsos, Jesus works at the
opposite end, finding a way to regain unity with God and

creation, and thereby make available and manifest that unity to all people. Satan attempts to make Jesus into any kind of clichéd epic hero, and Jesus has to use all the awareness he has: he rejects ordinary epic action and appears passive in Satan's eyes, in order to fulfill himself.

The glory temptation is the most explicit expression of this issue. The word has a rich biblical meaning,[8] now lapsed into obscurity, which provides Milton a ready focus on the two styles of heroism. In the Old Testament, the glory of the Lord is the "luminous splendor of his Presence, as though the Glory is his 'body,' " and that meaning persists in the New Testament to shape the understanding of Jesus' witness. By glory, the Bible usually means "the revealing of God's presence." That is what Milton means by his consistent descriptions of the Son as one in whom all his Father shone, and by means of Jesus this power becomes available to everyone. In Colossians, for example, Paul elaborates the reconciling work of Christ and of his own mission to his congregation:

> To whom God would make known what is the riches of the glory of this mystery among the Gentiles; which is Christ in you, the hope of glory: Whom we preach, warning every man, and teaching every man in all wisdom; that we may present every man perfect in Christ Jesus. [Col. 1:27–28]

The indwelling of God, or of Christ in each believer, is the experience of glory, which is the opposite of the desperate burden of egotism under which Satan labors. Glory in the worldly sense is always divisive, self-seeking, and therefore destructive.

Satan is wonderfully ironic, and blasphemous, in his description of God's desire for glory, which he vents in order to show Jesus that glory must be all right, since God insists on having so much of it:

> Think not so slight of glory; therein least
> Resembling thy great Father: he seeks glory,
> And for his glory all things made, all things
> Orders and governs, nor content in Heaven
> By all his Angels glorifi'd, requires
> Glory from men, from all men good or bad,
> Wise or unwise, no difference, no exemption;
> Above all Sacrifice, or hallow'd gift
> Glory he requires, and glory he receives
> Promiscuous from all Nations, Jew, or Greek,
> Or Barbarous, nor exception hath declar'd;
> From us his foes pronounc't glory he exacts.
>
> [3.109–20]

In Satan's quantifying mind, glory seems like a huge, universal, and senseless income tax, extorted from men by God. It is one place in the poem where Jesus responds with fervor, first defining the giving of glory to God simply as thanks for the good of creation, and then as a process whereby creation itself is raised to glory:

> Yet so much bounty is in God, such grace,
> That who advance his glory, not thir own,
> Them he himself to glory will advance.
>
> [3.142–44]

Yet, as so often in this poem, the process is the acceptance of power already there:

> Shall I seek glory then, as vain men seek
> Oft not deserv'd? I seek not mine, but his
> Who sent me, and thereby witness whence I am.
>
> [3.105–7]

Self-expression is God-expression, the wholehearted sub-mission of the self to the source of life.

All father-son relationships in epic are important. Seek-ing his father, the hero seeks to know and then to transcend himself, and to transcend time while still working within its confines. The first of Milton's two epics is primarily a consideration of the task of the father, and the second that of the son. The first affirms the value of creation even at the price of death and evil; the second affirms the possibil-ity of fulfilled life in a world of death. At the level of con-sciousness available to the Son through his oneness with life, those death-dealing forces become impotent and ir-relevant.

In most epic poems, it is clear that the son goes beyond the place where his own father stops. The God of *Paradise Lost*, Book 3, saw his own limitations, and gave up sov-ereignty to the Son for the sake of a renewal of life after the fall. Because of the fall, humanity became subject to external things, and it has been Jesus' task, as a man, to achieve freedom from that subjection. In the unique mir-roring of these particular epics, then, Jesus has renounced the sovereignty which in *Paradise Lost* Satan seized over the world, which has long possessed humanity, and which has been mistaken for godlike authority.

Jesus has come to free humanity from the Old Testa-ment law, and in that sense too he may be seen to have gone beyond his Father as Jehovah. But the most impor-tant difference between the two poems is the extent to which a transcendent God has shrunk in importance com-pared to the God immanent in Jesus. It is a notable dem-onstration of the movement in this direction that theology has taken since the sixteenth century. However, since God, beyond his local manifestations, is a force for life, he is never superseded but only furthered.

In his extensive retraction of the epic apparatus in this poem, the poet almost absents himself. He is the one, he says, with remarkable understatement, who "e're while the happy Garden sung." Then he exits, shortly to be followed by God. The Spirit will inspire, as wont, the "prompted Song else mute," but "prompted else mute," and borne "through highth or depth of natures bounds" seems a long way from "adventrous Song, / That with no middle flight intends to soar / Above th'Aonian Mount." The deeds now to be told are unrecorded, done in secret, and, in another understatement, "Worthy t'have not remain'd so long unsung."

The poet's reticent and sober style sets responsibility for what happens almost entirely upon the two main characters. It emphasizes the fallen state of the world and God's shift from transcendence to immanence. It forces the reader to look within for Paradise. Yet what can he mean by saying the story is "Worthy t'have not remain'd so long unsung"? Did the Apostles miss things? Even as a question, that seems almost a blasphemous suggestion. One might look, for an answer, to the new episodes and the refocusing of the story, even, perhaps, to the fact that he chooses this story rather than the Crucifixion as the regaining of Eden. Beyond these matters, there is the fact that this epic cannot be sung at all in the old way. What happens within Jesus is not described, nor is the glory that he radiates. These can be pointed at, but not set forth. The poem makes a heavy demand on the reader, whose task is to recognize what Milton cannot fully express, and what for so many ages has not been appreciated. To have the epic tradition behind him, at least to be able to say that compared to this epic tale, all others pall, ought to make all the difference. Too often it has simply caused critics to believe that Milton overrated his poem.

At the time when he was first preparing to write the great epic, when he thought of Arthurian combat, or that purer tale of the triumph of the English nation, to be sung on the shores of the commonwealth's Red Sea, he expected Utopia and a land of poetry unimaginably exquisite—a reward for the patient sorting out of gold from straw. But he now understood that Utopia could not be externally created. The pattern of Jesus had to be asserted in its obscurity, not in its triumph, and *Paradise Regained* was a rewriting of the "Nativity Ode" from a fallen perspective. This epic would spew out as much as it cannibalized, as the poet presents a hero who refuses to help the hungry or clothe the naked, raise up the humble, or cast down the proud.

Milton had once thought that the merest encouragement would open the grateful mind to its true freedom. The war taught him that he was wrong, and in three successive poems he described the lengths to which the mind will go to avoid opening itself to God. But in *Paradise Regained* he also provided a pattern to show that the possibility of salvation is there. The things of this world, potent as they are, can be overcome, but only, he repeats, by patient faith and fortitude. Looking for a savior may lead one into the clutches of the enemy. The eyes and ears of faith are meant for distinguishing the look-alikes of the world from one another.

Paradise Regained is designed like a dance. It would be incorrect to say that Jesus and Satan need one another. But

Satan has permission to try Jesus long enough for the Son to face and expel his dark self. In this dance of life, Satan and Jesus are so closely locked together as to seem indistinguishable without the eyes of faith. Like all epics, this poem does have a story line. More than in most epics, its contemplative line is also apparent. Milton takes care not to distract us too much, with the story, from the interlocked ballet of Satan and Jesus. He refuses to separate the books or characters with any distinctive rhetoric, he consistently resorts to anticlimax, he does not allow Jesus to develop in a humanly familiar way. He asks us simply to contemplate that stark ballet, two figuers in seemingly endless tension between the material and spiritual goods of the world, and to recognize what that tension really is, how devastating it can be when it seems to require the spiritual man to refuse compassion to those who are in sorrow, need, hunger, or any other adversity. Fair ladies in distress and knights deprived of their horses are not even worthy of mention. Jesus says that slaves are their own victims, and hunger its own cause, and he will not be compromised.

Later that stance will be of obvious help. The kinds of choices that he will make outside the poem, which may seem frivolous then—turning water into wine at a wedding, for instance—can be made without reference to any principle because he has learned self-mastery and can trust his instincts not to betray him for a momentary whim. But all that is later, and Milton does not make it a part of his pleading, which is wholly uncompromised.

The ballet is between good and evil. Because Jesus does not exhibit anxiety about a future in time, action and contemplation are absolutely united. Milton's story is that of a struggle in the desert which is without beginning or end, and yet begins and ends at every point. At no moment in the proceedings does it matter to Jesus whether Satan returns; at no moment is the struggle less than crucial. It does not gather momentum. The reason for its intensity is that it summarizes all light and all darkness. It is waged in total ignorance and in total awareness. Burton Weber's *Wedges and Wings* demonstrates that each temptation contains within itself each other temptation.[9] That is another means by which each moment is made self-complete. The typological nature of the characters also makes each moment whole. Even though Jesus and Satan do not entirely understand the truth of it, the fact that it has all happened before—in Heaven—makes chronology irrelevant. The fact that the characters at every moment do what they are (Jesus stands, Satan falls) makes chronology irrelevant.

At the end, both everything and nothing has happened:

> True Image of the Father, whether thron'd
> In the bosom of bliss, and light of light
> Conceiving, or remote from Heaven, enshrin'd
> In fleshly Tabernacle, and human form,
> Wandring the Wilderness, whatever place,
> Habit, or state, or motion, still expressing
> The Son of God, with Godlike force indu'd
> Against th'Attempter of thy Fathers Throne,
> And Thief of Paradise; him long of old
> Thou didst debel, and down from Heav'n cast
> With all his Army, now thou hast aveng'd
> Supplanted *Adam*, and by vanquishing
> Temptation, hast regain'd lost Paradise,
> And frustrated the conquest fraudulent:

He never more henceforth will dare set foot
In Paradise to tempt; his snares are broke:
For though that seat of earthly bliss be fail'd,
A fairer Paradise is founded now
For *Adam* and his chosen Sons, whom thou
A Saviour art come down to re-install.
Where they shall dwell secure, when time shall be
Of Tempter and Temptation without fear.
But thou, Infernal Serpent, shalt not long
Rule in the Clouds; like an Autumnal Star
Or Lightning thou shalt fall from Heav'n trod down
Under his feet: for proof, e're this thou feel'st
Thy wound, yet not thy last and deadliest wound
By this repulse receiv'd, and hold'st in Hell
No triumph; in all her gates *Abaddon* rues
Thy bold attempt; hereafter learn with awe
To dread the Son of God: he all unarm'd
Shall chase thee with the terror of his voice
From thy Demoniac holds, possession foul,
Thee and thy Legions, yelling they shall flye,
And beg to hide them in a herd of Swine,
Lest he command them down into the deep
Bound, and to torment sent before thir time.
Hail Son of the most High, heir of both worlds,
Queller of Satan, on thy glorious work
Now enter, and begin to save mankind.

[4.596–635]

In these remarkable lines, both space and time are of in-
finite importance and of no importance at all. The Son is
everywhere. He has warred, and has yet to war down
Satan. Paradise is regained and Satan's power canceled, as
if it had never been; Satan still rules and is yet to be cast
out. His snares are broken, but Jesus has not begun to save

mankind. The Son is everyman and the battle is within.

In discussion of previous epics, I have spoken of a momentary transcendence which may occur at any highly significant moment, but which is often identical with epic embrace, the union of opposites at the end of the poem. This poem and *Paradise Lost* are different from most epics because their intent is to understand the source and need for such oppositions and to transcend them. Jesus in this poem more fully succeeds in self-integration than any previous epic character. He completely apprehends and disdains the negative or destructive aspects of himself represented by Satan. The discords of the world, as male-female, day-night, rule-submission, are so integrated within him, and so fully submitted to the wholeness of his God-consciousness, that specific external things exercise no destructive pull upon him. It is his nature to be one.

It is important to our appreciation of our own heritage to recognize the specific means by which he does fulfill himself, for he makes a virtue of the consciousness that has come to seem so burdensome to many westerners. The power of discernment given to Christians of the early church provides a link between reason and intuition that enables Jesus to see clearly the difference between Satan's kingdom and the one meant for humanity. Such charismatic tools as these are means for the regaining of Paradise. So is the reminder that the soul is the image of God, which means that glory is within.

In this poem, as in *Paradise Lost*, the embrace is not between God or the Son and Satan, although that is what previous epics might have led us to expect. Milton distinguishes between the imperfection inherent in creation and the destructive urge that is Satan. Satan has continually to be cast off, so that creation can take place. The process of creation makes eternity possible both in the moment and in itself. In his wholeness the Son demonstrates what the embrace briefly achieves.[10] All who want life receive it through him, becoming one with him. And he unites God with humanity in the anticipation of his return to the embrace of God mentioned in the angelic hymn sung before his return to his mother's house.

Afterword

It has become a commonplace of modern criticism that Milton ended the epic tradition,[1] by writing in so unanswerable a style, or by burlesquing epic conventions, or by raising his major scenes and characters beyond human reach. In fact, by recognizing the senselessness of asking a modern epic to perpetuate such conventions as the use of classical gods and by reworking all the old characteristics to suit his own purposes, he was only following the transformational tradition of the genre. In contrast, other Renaissance epic poets waste energy and talent trying to "antique" their work, as Spenser did, or otherwise to maintain intact what they take to be necessary features—as with Camoens' two sets of deities.

But to answer the charges against Milton in such specific terms as these, while it can be useful, is to evade the more ruinous argument that epic itself is obsolete. Critics who have no intention of blaming Milton for its demise nevertheless agree that it has no place in modern literature. It is supposed to have been the form of a simpler, more coherent age, when man and his environment were so at one that symbolism was impossible. This argument denies the central character of epic, which exists to record and perhaps to create changes in human consciousness.

Whether or not it is true that no great epic poetry has

been written since Milton's, the present study proposes a reason for its absence. The length of time between epic poems that endure is often a matter of hundreds of years, because until one epic poem can no longer adequately describe its world, there is almost no possibility that another will be created. And even then, a writer of magnitude and prophetic power has to coincide with a major crisis or turning point in human consciousness and human culture. The burden or excitement of Milton's work, felt by so many major poets down to our own time, is an indication that he has had a continuing influence, inescapable because of its real value. Although men have chafed against the power of his poetry, that power has not represented the dead hand of the past, but the living force of a mind in combat with the sterility and materialism of our own society.

From its inception the epic concerns itself with the nature of human consciousness and its relation to "outer" and "physical" reality. With the Renaissance, problems of the existence, meaning, and interrelationships of inner and outer lives become both more articulated and more critical than ever before, as the center of human meaning shifts both in metaphor and in fact to the individual human being. Classical epic provides Milton with all the materials that he needed—that is to say, with a form which could be both active and contemplative, which could give the hero a necessary and communal task, while at the same time demonstrating that he could not perform it without the self-knowledge and the mortal knowledge that are more important than the task itself.

Milton questioned the reason for the task. Having experienced the epic victory of the Puritan cause followed by its apparent failure in the Restoration, he knew that the physical action of the heroic poem was no more important than his predecessors said it was; but then he wanted to know why it should be done at all. He is the theologian of the epic line. He chose, not the story of his time, but the original story that should explain all others. Adam and Eve had lost the perfect union of outer and inner reality, and thereby committed their descendants to history, and to actions which had to be accepted, but which would often distract them from their most important quest of self-knowledge.

The gorgeous rhetoric and the vast story of *Paradise Lost* are thus both necessary and suspect. No less is adequate to tell what must be known, but in the process of telling it begins to fall apart. Raphael is uncertain how to explain the correspondence between Heaven and earth. Almost all language concerning God is totally misleading. All of Satan's language is false, and the war in Heaven is as absurd as it is sublime. Milton tells us that the whole enterprise is valueless unless the story really comes to him from the muse. The language of external things is at best inadequate to describe spiritual reality. The true nature of epic is to praise patience and heroic fortitude, virtues which in *Paradise Lost* are not greatly in evidence.

Paradise Lost balances creation against destruction at the center of its pattern. At the same time, the major human action of the poem concerns the unmaking of a world. Its purpose is to forerun all epic, and to explain that heroic endeavor, of the sort henceforth to be portrayed, only occurs because men are fallen. At the same time it argues that heroism existed in the original involvement of Deity with creation. Thus it both deprecates and increases the value of the genre. It explains the hero's flaw, and also the necessity of his redemption through epic story. There is no epic that does not in some way carry the same intention. Whether the fall of Troy, the loss of Jerusalem, or the loss of Paradise is its symbol, epic is a story of loss and of attempted renewal. The strangeness of *Paradise Lost* is only in its explicit rationalization of the enterprise.

The characteristic epic action of loss and renewal may occupy two poems, as in the *Iliad* and the *Odyssey*, or one, as in the *Aeneid*, which consciously combines the two Greek poems. Following Homer here, as in so many things, Milton spends two poems on the pattern. *Paradise Lost* ends an era, as the *Iliad* does, or as the first half of the *Aeneid* does. In *Paradise Regained*, Jesus and Satan illustrate the opposite uses that modern man might make, or has made, of the modern world. If Eden was turned into a salt island, then Jesus would begin there, with no further attempt to glorify outer endurance and dominion. He rejects all the traditional goals of the epic hero by recognizing them as mere distractions from the human need for self-knowledge and self-control.

Satan is an alienated technocrat who has made the modern world into a desert of external things. Perhaps Milton foresaw the trivialization of epic action in a mechanized society. At any rate, one reason and technique for the diminution of Satan in *Paradise Regained* is that instead of making cosmic voyages of discovery, he now plays word-tricks and magic tricks, makes the desert bloom, provides panoramic views through telescopes, and dispenses funds for the subornation of armies and kingdoms. Scientific discoveries affirm the futility, or unimportance, of physical prowess. But where the external state of things provides

Ariosto's reason for cynicism, it merely corroborates beliefs Milton had maintained from the beginning. As the Renaissance turned from faith in medieval hierarchies supported by scholastic reasoning to faith in science supported by experimentation, Milton remained committed to faith first and foremost in a self-knowledge uncorrupted by surfaces. One of the foremost intellectuals of his time, he idolized nothing, not even learning, and one can see accordingly how fully even God has been internalized in the course of the two epics. Neither science nor any other kind of good is to be rejected, but they are meant to serve and not to command. Milton foresaw our contemporary problems of technology, sexism, indifferent power, and senseless nationalism, and demonstrated in his Jesus a way of avoiding all these traps.

Milton made the epic interior: Jesus descends into himself. Once this has happened, the way is open for the subjective hero to take any kind of interior journey.[2] Wishing to write their own epics, Blake, Wordsworth, and Shelley acknowledged Milton as their forebear. Yet once this line has been established, I believe that one is bound to feel a certain amount of uneasiness. At once internalized and impersonalized in Milton's poems, God is still a very present force for life, and a means by which alienation is totally overcome as outer and inner meaning become one. When Satan scornfully asks Jesus what he is doing in this world, that is because the two of them simply do not know the world in the same way. For Satan it consists of opportunities not to be missed. For Jesus it is part of a process leading back to God in God's own time.

Milton has argued in these two poems that evil can be rejected without any loss of power. God and Jesus both reject Satan while maintaining in themselves the cosmic authority that makes the reader believe in the continuing force of creation. Yet with the rejection of Satan in *Paradise Regained,* and the lessening presence of a transcendent God, the way opens for the entirely man-centered universe of contemporary poetry. The discoveries of modern psychology having corroborated what the poets always knew about the depths of the human spirit, there is still plenty of room for voyages of discovery. There is also room for solipsism and despair, in the absolute severing of the bond between outer and inner being.

We live in a time of political, economic, intellectual, and social crisis as deep as any previously known in human history. The sicknesses Milton names are ours. Our consciousness is desperate to pierce beyond itself into a more creative and spacious kind of awareness. The lack of a modern epic (and our belief in the obsolescence of the form) is as symptomatic as our lack of faith in anything else. Until the problems of Milton's poems are no longer familiar to us, we can scarcely demand another major epic, nor can we afford to say that his is obsolete. At the same time, it would be as well if we also did not assume that he ended the epic line. Our time, like his, has seen the feverish rise and fall of many strange gods and new religions, many false prophets. But, as Milton tells us, truth takes strange and unrecognizable shapes. We have been warned sufficiently to know that epic does that too. Against the solipsism which *Paradise Regained* seems both to encourage and to refute, it may be possible to raise a new kind of epic in a new heroic language for our age.

Notes

Quotations from Milton are from Frank Allen Patterson et al., eds., *The Works of John Milton* (18 vols. in 22; New York: Columbia University Press, 1931–38), and are identified parenthetically in the text.

For the poets of the tradition, the following editions were used, and quotations are identified parenthetically in the text:

The "Iliad" of Homer, trans. Richmond Lattimore (Chicago: University of Chicago Press, 1961).

The "Odyssey" of Homer, trans. Richmond Lattimore (New York: Harper and Row, 1965).

The "Aeneid" of Virgil, trans. Allen Mandelbaum (paperback ed.; New York: Bantam Books, 1971).

The "Divine Comedy" of Dante Alighieri: Italian Text with English Translation, trans. John D. Sinclair (3 vols.; rev. ed.; New York: Oxford University Press, 1961).

Quotations from Ludovico Ariosto, *Orlando Furioso,* are taken from the translation by Richard Hodgens (New York: Ballantine Books, 1973), which includes the first thirteen cantos. William Stewart Rose's translation of the complete work, which first appeared between 1823 and 1831, can be found in a modern edition edited by Stewart A. Baker and A. Bartlett Giametti (Indianapolis: Bobbs-Merrill Company, 1968).

Torquato Tasso, *Jerusalem Delivered,* trans. Edward Fairfax (1624), ed. John Charles Nelson (New York: Capricorn Books, 1963).

Luiz De Camoens, *The Lusiads,* trans. William C. Atkinson (Baltimore: Penguin Books, 1952).

Edmund Spenser, *The Faerie Queene,* ed. J. C. Smith (2 vols.; London: Oxford University Press, 1909).

The Tradition

1. I make the usual assumption that since subsequent literary epics refer back to Homer he must be included in the tradition, even though, if one is distinguishing between literary and folk, he is generally placed in the latter category. Although I have excluded "folk" epic from this study, I have not done so because of any strong belief in that distinction; in fact, most of the characteristics of these poems can be found in *Gilgamesh* and *Beowulf.* My original intention was to provide an epic context for *Paradise Lost* and *Paradise Regained* which Milton himself would have accepted.

2. Brian Wilkie, *Romantic Poets and Epic Tradition* (Madison: University of Wisconsin Press, 1965), p. 4.

3. Northrop Frye, *Anatomy of Criticism* (1957; paperback ed., Princeton, N.J.: Princeton University Press, 1971), pp. 55–58 and *passim.*

4. A number of critics have considered epic in this way. See, for example, Rosalie Colie, *The Resources of Kind,* ed. Barbara Lewalski (Berkeley and Los Angeles: University of California Press, 1973), and Joseph A. Wittreich, Jr., " 'A Poet amongst Poets': Milton and the Tradition of Prophecy," in *Milton and the Line of Vision* (Madison: University of Wisconsin Press, 1975), pp. 102–3, 129–31.

5. Joseph A. Wittreich, Jr., *Angel of Apocalypse: Blake's Idea of Milton* (Madison: University of Wisconsin Press, 1975), p. 168.

6. Wittreich, " 'A Poet amongst Poets,' " p. 102; and *Visionary Poetics: Milton's Tradition and His Legacy* (San Marino, Calif.: Huntington Library, 1979), esp. pp. 3–78.

7. Wilkie, *Romantic Poets and Epic Tradition,* p. 5.

8. Angus Fletcher, who has made this term current in Renaissance criticism, defines it circularly: a transcendental form is one

that exceeds the limits of the genre (*The Transcendental Masque: An Essay on Milton's Comus* [Ithaca, N.Y.: Cornell University Press, 1971], p. 116). Such a definition may seem absurd, but, with regard to epic, it is also accurate, and consistent with such requirements as that all significant epics must include other genres as well as other epics, and that they must be great.

9. Wilkie, *Romantic Poets and Epic Tradition*, p. 14.

10. Laurence Stapleton, *The Elected Circle: Studies in the Art of Prose* (Princeton, N.J.: Princeton University Press, 1973).

11. "The Reason for Church-Government Urged against Prelaty," in Patterson et al., eds., *The Works of John Milton*, vol. 3, pt. 1, p. 237.

12. Erich Neumann, *The Origins and History of Consciousness* (first published in German, 1949), trans. R. F. Hull (Princeton N.J.: Princeton University Press, 1970); Erich Kahler, *The Inward Turn of Narrative* (first published in German, 1957), trans. Richard and Clara Winston (Princeton, N.J.: Princeton University Press, 1973). Since I have made some use of Neumann's work throughout this book, I should note my awareness that his ideas are controversial among Jungians, and that Neumann is probably wrong in some important respects, as in his association of the history of man with the growth of the individual person, and in his insistence on the literal historicity of specific stages of human development, including, for example, a matriarchal society. Nevertheless, Neumann is certainly right in some of his central insights, as in the description of the way in which consciousness has expanded its territory (which is my main argument here), in his description of the mother-son relationship, and, of course, in his assumption of the constant presence of certain fundamental archetypes in the human psyche, which vary importantly from one historical period, as well as from one human being, to another. Despite the uneven quality of his scholarship, it has seemed much more convenient to use this one book, where so much is brought together, than to cite the same information in scattered works of Jung, or to ignore altogether the existence of this important material.

13. Kahler, *The Inward Turn of Narrative*, p. 6.

14. As previously indicated, consciousness expands its territory. However, words like "expanded," used in this connection, are never intended to imply a value judgment, or an idealistic reading of history. Consciousness changes, but does not necessarily improve with time.

15. Several critics stress the importance of the sense of mortality in epic, among them Albert Cook, *The Classic Line: A Study in Epic Poetry* (Bloomington: Indiana University Press, 1966). Thomas Greene, in *The Descent from Heaven* (New Haven, Conn.: Yale University Press, 1963), p. 15, says that the hero's most important task is the acceptance of his own mortality.

16. Neumann, *The Origins and Hisory of Consciousness*, p. 14.

17. Thomas McFarland, in "Lykaon and Achilles," *Yale Review*, 45 (Winter 1956): 191–213, argues very persuasively that Achilles is angry because his only reason for fighting the war—the code of loyalty—has been ignorantly denied by Agamemnon. McFarland believes Achilles' intelligence and profundity of character to be greater than those of any of his fellow warriors, and while this may be an overstatement, I do not intend to belittle Achilles' intelligence by saying that it is inarticulate.

18. Charles H. Taylor, Jr., "Odysseus, the Inner Man," in *Homer's "Odyssey": A Critical Handbook*, ed. Conny Nelson (Belmont, Calif.: Wadsworth, 1969), pp. 18–27, discusses the *Odyssey* as struggle for individual consciousness, using much of the material discussed here.

19. Kahler, *The Inward Turn of Narrative*, p. 21.

20. On this, see Michael C. J. Putnam, *The Poetry of the "Aeneid"* (Cambridge, Mass.: Harvard University Press, 1965), p. 4. For an excellent recent study of the *Aeneid*, see Mario Di-Cesare, *The Altar and the City: A Reading of Vergil's "Aeneid"* (New York: Columbia University Press, 1974).

21. This change in consciousness is described by Neumann, *The Original History of Consciousness*, pp. 5–101.

22. Sometimes the sea attacks consciousness, or civilization. Troy was Neptune's city, but Neptune himself tore it down (*Aeneid*, 2:608–18). See also the figure of Adamastor in Camoens' *Lusiads*.

23. There are woods in the *Aeneid*, notably in Book 6, where it is unclear where the woods stop and the underworld begins. See Putnam, *The Poetry of the "Aeneid*," for this and other use of woods. Ernst Robert Curtius, *European Literature and the Latin Middle Ages* (first published in German, 1948), trans. Willard R. Trask (New York: Pantheon Books, 1953), p. 201, says the wild forest motif is primarily a creation of the French courtly romance.

24. Dante's letter to Can Grande, in Charles Sterrett Latham, *A Translation of Dante's Eleven Letters* (Boston: Houghton Mifflin, 1892), p. 195.

25. Torquato Tasso, "The Allegories of the Poem," in *Godfrey of Bologne, or The Recoverie of Jerusalem.*

Judith Kates argues that in devaluing classical epic devices, by assigning them to pagan warriors, Tasso prepares the way for Milton. She particularly stresses Tasso's emphasis on the classical ideal of individual heroism as a pagan attribute. However, personal honor was always in tension with the needs of the community, as was the elemental force of the pagan with the "civilization" of the hero. Kates's essay is worth reading, nevertheless, for its Miltonic insights into the earlier poem. See "The Revaluation of the Classical Heroic in Tasso and Milton," *Comparative Literature*, 26 (Fall 1974): 299–317.

26. See John Webster, "Language and Allegory in *The Faerie Queene*," Ph.D. diss., University of California, Berkeley, 1974.

27. But Mario DiCesare argues that they have echoed so positively only because they have been taken out of context (*The Altar and the City*, p. 119).

28. Peter Pope, "A Study of Tragedy in the Second Half of the *Aeneid*," essay written at Ohio State University, 1972. The extent to which Vergil intended his poem to undercut the idea of empire is an open question. The earliest and most strenuous attack on the conventional reading is that of Francesco Sforza in the *Classical Review*, 49 (1935): 97–108. Mario DiCesare's *The Altar and the City* is the most recent and fairest study.

29. Thomas Greene, *Descent from Heaven*, complains that Ariosto does not achieve epic, partly because he undermines the

church, mainspring of society, without replacing it with anything else. But that is just the point; that is what epic does, and Dante's capacity to find a better church is so unusual as to have called in question *his* right to epic stature.

30. The phrase is used by C. P. Brand, *Torquato Tasso* (Cambridge: Cambridge University Press, 1965), p. 85.

31. See Edward Dudley and Maximillian E. Novak, eds., *The Wild Man Within: An Image in Western Thought from the Renaissance to Romanticism* (Pittsburgh, Pa.: University of Pittsburgh Press, 1972), and Carol Elaine Dooley, "Salvage Man and Salvage Knight: Use of the Medieval Wild Man Motif in Edmund Spenser's *The Faerie Queene*" (Ph.D. diss., University of Washington, 1974).

32. For discussion of the concept of earthly paradise, see A. Bartlett Giamatti, *The Earthly Paradise and the Renaissance Epic* (Princeton, N.J.: Princeton University Press, 1965).

33. The noun "tragedy" denotes a genre; the adjective "tragic" denotes a *mythos*, in the terminology of Northrop Frye, who would consider "play," not "tragedy," a genre (*Anatomy of Criticism*). Confusing as it becomes to consider tragedy in both senses, I think it for all practical purposes impossible to relinquish the concept of tragedy (and allied terms, like comedy and romance) as a genre.

34. See Jerome Dees, "The Narrator of *The Faerie Queene*: Patterns of Response," *Texas Studies in Literature and Language*, 12 (Winter 1971): 537–68.

35. For discussion and bibliography, see Robert Ornstein, *The Psychology of Consciousness* (San Francisco: W. H. Freeman, 1972), p. 67.

36. On the Amazons, see Guy Cadogan Rothery, *The Amazons in Antiquity and Modern Times* (London: Francis Griffiths, 1910), and Donald J. Sobol, *The Amazons of Greek Mythology* (South Brunswick: A. S. Barnes, 1972).

37. On Penelope as goal, and feminine counterpart of Odysseus, and her importance to his wholeness, see Taylor, "Odysseus, the Inner Man," p. 27. See also Agatha Thornton, *People and Themes in Homer's "Odyssey"* (Dunedin: University of Otago Press, 1970), p. 10, commenting on the underworld scene in Book 24,

where Odysseus "emerges as the greatest" of the Greek heroes, "thanks to Penelope."

38. The poem often uses weaving as a metaphor for trickery (see Thornton, *People and Themes in Homer's "Odyssey,"* pp. 94–95), a fact which nicely connects the minds of Odysseus and Penelope.

39. Thomas Greene, *Descent from Heaven.*

40. See Wilkie, *Romantic Poets and Epic Tradition,* Chap. 1.

41. Thomas Maresca, in *Epic to Novel* (Columbus: Ohio State University Press, 1974), argues (rightly, I think) that mirroring is a defining characteristic of epic, and that it is an effort to repair the ruins of our first parents by confrontation of the crooked with the true, the journeying with the return, and so forth. See also Cedric H. Whitman, *Homer and the Heroic Tradition* (Cambridge, Mass.: Harvard University Press, 1958), pp. 249–84, and Brooks Otis, *Virgil: A Study in Civilized Poetry* (Oxford: Clarendon Press, 1963), Chaps. 6 and 7.

42. Robert Frost, *Complete Poems of Robert Frost* (New York: Henry Holt and Co., 1959), p. vi.

43. According to John Steadman, another word to describe the true goal of Christian epic is "felicity," or "beatitude." Surely, though, a kind of beatitude is achieved in pre-Christian moments of transcendence. Steadman's sense that beatitude is extrinsic to the poem in Tasso and Spenser, intrinsic in Milton, is clear enough, however, and provides further evidence that Milton always goes back to basic principles. See John M. Steadman, "Felicity and End in Renaissance Epic and Ethics," *Journal of the History of Ideas,* 23 (Jan.–Mar. 1962), pp. 117–32.

44. See, for example, *Mysterium Conjunctionis,* vol. 14 (1963), in *The Collected Works of C. G. Jung* (Princeton, N.J.: Princeton University Press, 1957–), trans. R. F. C. Hull, ed. Sir Herbert Read, Michael Fordham, and Gerhard Adler.

Paradise Lost

1. For discussion of these images, see Thomas Kranidas, *The Fierce Equation: A Study of Milton's Decorum* (The Hague: Mouton and Co., 1965).

2. Torquato Tasso, *Discourses on the Heroic Poem,* trans. Mariella Cavalchini and Irene Samuel (Oxford: Clarendon Press, 1973), p. 37.

3. See Thomas Kranidas, *The Fierce Equation;* and Joan Webber, *The Eloquent 'I': Style and Self in Seventeenth-Century Prose* (Madison: University of Wisconsin Press, 1968).

4. William Riley Parker, *Milton: A Biography* (2 vols.; Oxford: Clarendon Press, 1968), 1:593.

5. Ibid., pp. 600–1.

6. For more extensive discussion, see my essay, "Milton's God," *ELH*, 40 (Winter 1973): 514–31. The more time I spend thinking about Milton's God, the more difficult it seems to me to take any kind of exclusive approach to his definition. Simply, God cannot be defined. Neither a strictly historical, orthodox theological context, nor one, like mine, which comes from the style of the poem and its poet and muse, can wholly satisfy. Although that is hard on the critic, it seems right that if Milton has succeeded, then his God should defy language.

7. On the eligibility of gods as heroes, see pp. 47–48. It is the literal involvement of God and human beings in one another that makes it possible in Christianity for God to become man and man to become one with God.

8. On the theology of creation, see J. H. Adamson, "The Creation," in *Bright Essence: Studies in Milton's Theology,* by W. B. Hunter, C. A. Patrides, and J. H. Adamson (Salt Lake: University of Utah Press, 1971), pp. 81–102; Walter Clyde Curry, *Milton's Ontology, Cosmogony, and Physics* (Lexington: University of Kentucky Press, 1957); A. B. Chambers, "Chaos in *Paradise Lost,*" *Journal of the History of Ideas,* 24 (1963): 55–84; and Michael Lieb, *The Dialectics of Creation: Patterns of Birth and Regeneration in "Paradise Lost"* (Amherst: University of Massachusetts Press, 1970). The two major commentators on Milton's theological treatise, *De Doctrina Christiana,* are Maurice Kelley, *This Great Argument: A Study of Milton's "De Doctrina Christiana" as a Gloss upon "Paradise Lost,"* Princeton Studies in English, 22 (Princeton, N.J.: Princeton University Press, 1941), and C. A. Patrides, *Milton and the Christian Tradition* (Oxford:

Clarendon Press, 1966). Patrides, rightly I think, argues that the theology of *Paradise Lost* is freer and more "modern" than that of *De Doctrina*. See C. A. Patrides, *"Paradise Lost* and the Language of Theology," in *Language and Style in Milton,* ed. Ronald Emma and John T. Shawcross (New York: Ungar, 1967), pp. 102–19. For further discussion, see my "Milton's God."

9. See my essay, "The Son of God and Power of Life in Three Poems by Milton," *ELH,* 37 (June 1970): 175–94.

10. This is pointed out by Northrop Frye in *The Return of Eden: Five Essays in Milton's Epics* (Toronto: University of Toronto Press, 1965), p. 99. He solves the problem of Milton's God by making him equivalent to the image of God in the soul. He represents inner, not outer authority, the self-discipline that Milton had always thought prerequisite to government of others, and which became paramount for him when revolutionary government failed. But Frye also accepts the existence of an outer authority in heaven, which is eventually to be discarded.

Yet another possible way of thinking about God, which could explain his sense of humor without necessarily diminishing him, is given in the Book of Revelation, where the war in Heaven is merely a phase in a long-standing antagonism between God and Satan, here resolved. The timelessness essential to this theory is already a part of *Paradise Lost.* "And I heard a loud voice saying in heaven, Now is come salvation, and strength, and the kingdom of our God, and the power of his Christ: for the accuser of our brethren is cast down, which accused them before our God day and night. . . . Therefore rejoice, ye heavens, and ye that dwell in them. Woe to the inhabiters of the earth and of the sea! for the devil is come down unto you, having great wrath, because he knoweth that he hath but a short time" (Revelation 12.10, 12).

11. See Laurie Zwicky, "Kairos in *Paradise Regained:* The Divine Plan," *ELH,* 31 (1964): 271–77.

12. Of the twenty-four occurrences of the words in *Paradise Lost,* eight are in these passages. See William Ingram and Kathleen Swaim, eds., *A Concordance to Milton's English Poetry* (Oxford: Clarendon Press, 1972).

13. See Don Parry Norford, " 'My other half': The Coinci-

dence of Opposites in *Paradise Lost*," *Modern Language Quarterly*, 36 (March 1975): 21–53.

14. Milton is unusual among Puritans in his lack of despair, in the absence, in his autobiographical accounts, of descriptions of distrust, despair, or conversion. Only the emphasis on patience, possibly his defenses of himself (though these are rhetorically conventional), and this one passage in *Paradise Lost* could be used to suggest uncertainty.

15. See Barbara Lewalski, "Innocence and Experience in Milton's Eden," in *New Essays on "Paradise Lost,"* ed. Thomas Kranidas (Berkeley and Los Angeles: University of California Press, 1969).

16. Bartholomew Keckermann, in *Rhetoricae Ecclesiasticae Sive Artis Formandi et Habendi Concieones Sacras* (3rd ed.; Hanau, 1606), p. 47. Erasmus makes a similar distinction between *scire* and *sapere,* in *Ecclesiastes: Opera Omnia* (Leiden, 1703–6), vol. 5, col. 777B.

17. See Albert W. Fields, "Milton and Self-Knowledge," *PMLA,* 83 (May 1968): 392–99.

18. Stanley E. Fish, *Surprised by Sin: The Reader in "Paradise Lost"* (Berkeley and Los Angeles: University of California Press, 1971).

19. Norford, " 'My other half.' "

20. Christopher Ricks, *Milton's Grand Style* (Oxford: Clarendon Press, 1963), pp. 139–40. Ricks quotes Charles Williams at length, from his Introduction to *The English Poems of Milton* (London: Oxford University Press, 1940), p. xix, and also refers to Kester Svendsen, *Milton and Science* (Cambridge, Mass.: Harvard University Press, 1956).

21. See W. B. Hunter, "Milton's Muse," in *Bright Essence,* pp. 149–56.

22. William G. Riggs, *The Christian Poet in "Paradise Lost"* (Berkeley and Los Angeles: University of California Press, 1972).

23. See William Kerrigan, *The Prophetic Milton* (Charlottesville: University Press of Virginia, 1974), and Joseph A. Wittreich, Jr., *Angel of Apocalypse: Blake's Idea of Milton* (Madison: University of Wisconsin Press, 1975).

24. John Steadman, *Milton and the Renaissance Hero* (Oxford: Clarendon Press, 1967), Chap. 8, "The Revaluation of Epic Tradition," pp. 177–201.

25. See Kerrigan, *The Prophetic Milton;* Michael Fixler, "The Apocalypse within *Paradise Lost,*" in *New Essays on "Paradise Lost,*" ed. Kranidas; Wittreich, *Angel of Apocalypse;* William Haller, *The Elect Nation: The Meaning and Relevance of Foxe's "Book of Martyrs"* (New York, 1963).

26. Thomas Maresca's *Epic to Novel* (Columbus: Ohio State University Press, 1974), which I saw only after this manuscript was complete, argues for a pattern of mirroring which he considers intrinsic to epic poetry, and which reflects the restoration of providential order after disruption. He points out that in *Paradise Lost* all things, badly or well, mirror God, and works out a scheme of reflective balance among the books of the poem. I believe that Maresca sees the epic as more self-enclosed and conservative than I do: however, our findings certainly corroborate each other in showing that reflexivity is a central means by which epic expresses itself.

Paradise Regained

1. Documentation in this section will be intentionally light. Almost every line of the poem has received extensive commentary from previous critics, although full-length studies of *Paradise Regained* are few in comparison to *Paradise Lost,* and the poem is short enough so that readers will remember the previous arguments. Also, Burton Weber's *Wedges and Wings* proceeds by means of considering previous arguments, and scholars wishing this information can easily find it there. The major books on *Paradise Regained* are as follows:

Elizabeth Pope, *"Paradise Regained": The Tradition and the Poem* (Baltimore, Md.: Johns Hopkins University Press, 1947).

Arnold Stein, *Heroic Knowledge: An Interpretation of "Paradise Regained" and "Samson Agonistes"* (Minneapolis: University of Minnesota Press, 1947).

Barbara K. Lewalski, *Milton's Brief Epic: The Genre, Meaning, and Art of "Paradise Regained"* (Providence, R.I.: Brown University Press, 1966).

Burton Jasper Weber, *Wedges and Wings: The Patterning of "Paradise Regained"* (Carbondale: Southern Illinois University Press, 1975).

2. William Riley Parker, *Milton: A Biography* (2 vols.; Oxford: Clarendon Press, 1968), 1:616, cites this remark, but questions its accuracy; he thinks that some lines were composed as early as 1665.

3. I think that Arnold Stein first pointed this out in *Heroic Knowledge*, pp. 6–7. The allusion recalls the probably inauthentic prologue to the *Aeneid*, accepted in Milton's time.

4. On this use of the phrase, see William Haller, *The Rise of Puritanism* (New York, 1938), p. 23. The source is 1 Cor. 1.17: "For Christ sent me not to baptize, but preach the gospel: not with wisdom of words, lest the cross of Christ should be made of none effect." It was cited by Christian rhetoricians from Augustine on.

5. The passage in Cassian is cited by Hugo Rahner, in *Ignatius the Theologian* (first published in German, 1964), trans. Michael Barry (London: G. Chapman, 1968), p. 176.

6. Jacques Guillet et al., *Discernment of Spirits*, trans. Sister Innocentia Richards (Collegeville, Miss.: Liturgical Press, 1970), p. 33.

7. Milton could have used the biblical episode in which Jesus is repeatedly accused of madness (having a devil) by the Jews, most emphatically because he seeks not his own glory but God's and because he promises that "if a man keep my saying, he shall never see death" (John 8.48–52).

8. For instance, Moses asks to see God's glory, by which he means "the full manifestation" of God's nature. Most of this information is given in *Peake's Commentary on the Bible*, ed. Matthew Black and H. H. Rowley (London: Thomas Nelson and Sons, 1962), 201j and 866b.

9. Burton Jasper Weber, *Wedges and Wings: The Patterning of Paradise Regained* (Carbondale: Southern Illinois University Press, 1975).

10. For his final illustration to *Paradise Regained*, Blake chose to visualize an embrace between Christ and his mother. It was a brilliant decision, entirely faithful to the epic, and one which Milton himself implies in the last line of the poem.

Afterword

1. See, for example, T. B. J. Spencer, *"Paradise Lost:* The Anti-Epic," in *Approaches to "Paradise Lost,"* ed. C. A. Patrides (Toronto: University of Toronto Press, 1968), p. 98: "The death of epic was, in Milton's hands, a glorious and perfectly staged suicide." For a magisterial statement to the contrary, see John Steadman, "The Revaluation of Epic Tradition," in *Milton and the Renaissance Hero* (Oxford: Clarendon Press, 1967).

2. Stuart Curran, "The Mental Pinnacle: *Paradise Regained* and the Romantic Four-Book Epic," in *Calm of Mind: Tercentenary Essays on "Paradise Regained" and "Samson Agonistes,"* ed. Joseph A. Wittreich (Cleveland, Ohio: Press of Case Western Reserve University, 1971), pp. 133–62. See also Brian Wilkie, *Romantic Poets and Epic Tradition* (Madison: University of Wisconsin Press, 1965); and Judith Kates, "The Revaluation of the Classical Heroic in Tasso and Milton," *Comparative Literature*, 26 (Fall 1974): 299–317.

Index

The following abbreviations have been used in the Index:

DC Divine Comedy
FQ Faerie Queene
JD Jerusalem Delivered

OF Orlando Furioso
PL Paradise Lost
PR Paradise Regained

Abel, 123
Abraham, 119
Abyss. *See* Chaos
Achilles: subject to temptations, 13-14; as epic hero, 39, 43, 155; violence of, 43-44; as subject of *Iliad*, 45; and Hector, 46; isolation of, 57; acceptance of mortality, 60; and art within *Iliad*, 63; and Priam, 82, 85, 97; and Agamemnon, 92, 124; mentioned, 48, 56, 69, 220n17. *See also* Homer; *Iliad*
Acidale, 94
Acrasia, 69, 70, 78
Action: and contemplation in epic, 44, 56, 91-94; and evil in *PL*, 145; in *PR*, 185
Adam: as hermaphroditic, 67; Michael's portrayal of history for, 122-23, 163; and Ra-

phael's account of creation of man, 124, 213; reaction after the Fall, 126, 150-51, 213; compared to Prometheus, 132; desire for knowledge, 132, 133-34, 182; self-consciousness of, 136; acceptance of mortality, 137-38; relationship to Eve, 138-39, 147-48
Adamastor, 30, 220n22
Aegisthus, 76
Aeneas: self-discipline of, 16-17, 18-19, 26, 43-44; compared to Odysseus, 18-19; protected by gods, 31; and Dido, 31, 58, 66, 75, 77; motivation of, 39-40; as model for later epic heroes, 43, 157, 190; violence of, 43, 58; as representing civilization, 46; as isolated

231